M000310179

There's *Someone*
in Your KINGDOM, Lord

Comfort & hope,

Jean

Isa. 43:1-3

There's *Someone* in Your KINGDOM, *Lord*

Jean Werth

Pleasant Word

© 2002 by Jean Werth. All rights reserved.
2nd printing in 2006

Printed in the United States of America.

Packaged by Pleasant Word, PO Box 428, Enumclaw, WA
98022. The views expressed or implied in this work do not
necessarily reflect those of WinePress Publishing. The author
is ultimately responsible for the design, content, and editorial
accuracy of this work.

Names mentioned in the text are used by permission.

No part of this publication may be reproduced, stored in a
retrieval system or transmitted in any way by any means,
electronic, mechanical, photocopy, recording or otherwise,
without the prior permission of the copyright holder except
as provided by USA copyright law.

All scripture quotations, unless otherwise indicated, are taken
from the Holy Bible, New International Version, copyright ©
1973, 1978, 1984 by the International Bible Society. Used by
permission of Zondervan Publishing House. The "NIV" and
"New International Version" trademarks are registered in the
United States Patent and Trademark Office by International
Bible Society.

Scripture references marked KJV are taken from the King James
Version of the Bible.

Dedication

This book is

> *written in memory of our precious son, Stephen Paul, who entered heaven at the age of thirteen and is now living with our Savior.*

This book is

> *dedicated to my husband, Gerry, whose love, faith, comfort, and encouragement have been a source of strength throughout my life;*

> *and to my two sons, Bill and Dave, who have brought me much joy and have shown me the path to a closer relationship with our Heavenly Father.*

This book is

> *written for anyone who is mourning the loss of a child and struggles on the day-to-day journey toward healing and hope.*

Acknowledgments

I must mention a number of people without whose help and support this book could not have been written. These people gave their time to answer questions and provide input. Their responses came with sincerity, honesty, and in all cases, heartfelt sadness. Knowing that the interviews would not be easy, they still welcomed me into their homes and conveyed events that led up to the death of either their born or unborn children. We cried together and even laughed occasionally as we recalled memories of our children.

My deepest thank you to a dear friend, Manna Bruckner, who gave me insight into healing and still remains a role model for courage. Her son, Ben, was the same age as our son when he died, so our sorrow is similar in many ways. Glen and Jane Roehm spent hours with me as they recalled the death of their four-day-old daughter. Although she entered heaven seven years ago, her memory is carried on in this book. Becky Ashcraft gave a detailed account of what a parent goes through after waiting years for a special baby only to have that child die from SIDS. Bobbie Lulos recalled the death of her twenty-year-old son and gave some wonderful ideas for coping as each day comes. Pam Roudebush sat for hours with me as she recalled the pain of miscarriage, a quiet loss but, nonetheless, painful. Her honesty gave me a greater understanding of the depth of pain parents endure whose lives have been touched by miscarriage. Cathy Terry attended one of the support groups offered through A Place That Warms the Heart in Shreveport. She freely shared her feelings about the loss of her six-year-old son, Mikey, and contributed greatly to the overall healing of the support group.

Two of our son's friends also consented to interviews. Mike Noffze and Chris Gerbers were very candid and open about their feelings and how our son's death affected their lives. Each recalled special times and happy memories. They both have experienced a sad time in their lives, and their information will comfort and support other young people going through the same tragedy.

Special thanks to Pastor and Mrs. James Cotter for all their prayers, support, input, and constant friendship through the most difficult time of our lives. They have felt the pain of multiple miscarriages, and this has given them a unique awareness of our pain. Betsy Williams, head of pastoral care at Christus Schumpert Health Center, suggested we use this book as the format for the support group for parents who had lost a child. This gave me an opportunity to see the effects of the material in a life setting.

Also I would like to express my sincere thanks to Randall Schroeder, Ph.D. for his counseling, his friendship, and most of all, his prayers. His guidance directed our family onto a path of strength and healing. We are all indebted to him for his Christian concern, help, and support.

Our son, David, drew the illustrations throughout the book. He expressed love for his brother, Stephen, using the wonderful talent God has given him. Each drawing creates a picture expressing a special memory for our family. His addition to my book is a loving tribute to his brother.

Contents

Weddings and Anniversaries,
Death of Other Family Members or Friends,
Following Activities of Your Child's Friends

Preface

The death of a child has been known to be the greatest pain any human can experience. Until we lost our son, I felt sorry for people who were going through the loss but did not come anywhere near grasping their devastation. When this tragedy touched our family, I turned to many sources for comfort. I tried to find information that would explain my pain and loss. My Bible became a source of hope and peace. I found, however, that I needed other literature to explain all the changes, the pangs of devastation, and flashes of what seemed insanity, which had become a part of my life.

A number of excellent books are available that explain therapeutic measures for grieving parents and friends, but I found nothing dealt with the everyday issues that hurt so badly—issues such as cleaning your child's room for the first time after his death, watching other children your child's age, celebrating holidays, etc. None seemed to address these to the extent I needed. Many of the authors had experienced the death of someone else's child but not their own. Therapists can provide extremely helpful counseling and, without them, our family may still be dangling in despair. But I felt that grieving parents needed a book written by a mother who could address the issues that were not found in psychology books; issues that dealt with the everyday matters of the brokenhearted.

I also wanted to provide a book that interspersed Scripture throughout for reference—passages that would provide comfort throughout the normal, everyday activity of a busy household. We know these passages are in the Bible, but taking time to reference them is sometimes hard for us to do. The Scripture included in these pages will help the reader get through many situations by simply reflecting on one passage at a time.

Throughout this book, when referring to the child who has died, I have used the male pronoun. I do so because of our specific case. As you read through this book, please use the pronoun that best reflects your situation.

This book is for parents, families, caregivers, clergy, and friends of children who have died. Members of families have provided sometimes painful but honest answers to questions of survival after miscarriages, stillborn births, and deaths of children. All these interviews, surprisingly, brought cleansing to the caverns of grief that, as yet, had not been dealt with. The couples I interviewed spoke freely of their child and the circumstances surrounding that child's death. The element of time since the death made absolutely no difference in the flow of tears that came freely during the interviews. Men and women were touched equally as they expressed their feelings and professed their faith. Friends who had lost friends, most of them teenagers, were very open and received an insight into the scope and direction of their life from the loss of their friend. As the interviews closed, I found that I also received strength from talking with each person. As is so often the case with those who grieve together, strength is drawn from each other through tears, words, hugs, and even smiles.

The first part of this book describes the circumstances that surrounded our son's death. It provides the basis for our grief as a family, and it is my hope that the reader will identify with our trauma and loss. The middle section is based on issues, family reflections, and special occasions and their role in our grieving process. The last portion is provided as a source of hope and anticipation for the future.

May this book provide the reader with acknowledgment, strength, and peace as we journey down the path of life until we see our loved ones again.

> Always be prepared to give an answer to everyone who asks you to give the reason for the hope that you have. (1 Pet. 3:15)

The Road to Heaven

Photo taken by Sue Hebel, Concordia Lutheran High School. Used with permission

The Road to Heaven

Yeah! Steve! Yeah! Steve!" The standing-room-only crowd at the Concordia Lutheran High School basketball game cheered rhythmically as the JROTC mascot rifle team took the floor for the half time demonstration. All the fans rose to their feet, clapping and shouting.

The mascot rifle team consisted of four junior and senior JROTC cadets performing a rifle drill demonstration. They performed each season, but this year an extra person marched with them, right in the middle of the circle. A twelve-year-old boy, dressed in full uniform, nervously but very proudly twirled a rifle that was almost as big as he was. His uniform had to be altered from the size that would fit a junior or senior student down to a boy's size 12. The shiny boots had received special care from hours of spit shining to bring a sparkle that would have challenged even his father's Corfams!

As they marched onto the floor, I tearfully watched from the top of the bleachers and couldn't help but ponder . . . *Stephen, if you have only one moment of glory in your life, if you live only a short time, this is the moment that will have brought you the greatest joy!* Little did I know that the next time Concordia played Bishop Dwenger Catholic High School on our home court, they would be praying at half time for everyone mourning the death of this little Christian soldier who had gone to be with his Lord.

It was just another Thursday morning, December 14, 1989. Stephen would not go to school today, however, because he had to have some minor surgery on his hand at the dermatologist. Gerry, my husband, would take him. When I finished work at noon, I would take Stephen to our favorite place for lunch. At 12:30 P.M. I got home, and the two of us went to McDonald's for our customary cheeseburger, fries, and a coke. We didn't do this very often, but when we did, I always enjoyed our time together because Stephen was a talker. He never failed to amuse me with his numerous questions and sense of humor.

He put a Batman video into the VCR when we got home and asked me to watch it with him. "I would like to, but I'm making fudge for Christmas and can't do it right now," I replied. How I wish now that I would have spent those few precious hours by his side, for that was the last request he made of me.

I finished the fudge and asked him to come and lick the spoon, a task he enjoyed thoroughly! Soon it was time for his brother, Dave, to come home from school. Steve jumped up to open the door as Dave drove up. Stephen idolized his older two brothers, as I'm sure all younger siblings do. He proceeded to give Dave the details of the movie, and the two of them laughed and wrestled on the family room floor. Stephen was becoming stronger as he got older and sometimes presented a challenge for his brother. This, of course, made the match much more enticing to Dave, who was very competitive. They didn't always get along this well, for they had their share of sibling rivalry episodes, but today they were best buddies.

That evening I would be going to choir practice at our church, and the boys would spend the time with Dad. Our oldest son, Bill, was in college so the evening would be just Dad and the two boys. As I was making supper, I remembered that my car needed gasoline. I asked Dave to drive one-quarter mile to the gas station to fill my tank. Stephen begged his brother to ride along. When Dave said yes, Stephen leaped off the couch before Dave could change his mind. He put on his winter coat, and out the door they went. I never had any trouble getting Dave to run errands for me because he liked driving my car. These excursions provided an opportunity for Dave and Steve to be out on their own in the car.

I always stood by the front window in our living room and prayed each time the boys drove away. Somehow I felt that this petition would envelope them with protection and return them safely home. This particular evening, however, I was busy preparing supper and did not go to the front window to pray.

They were gone about half an hour, and Gerry had returned home from his job at Grissom Air Force Base. Supper was ready, but the boys were not home. "I'll go to the gas station and see if something's wrong," Gerry offered. As he left, I mentioned, "If there's an accident, just tell the boys to wait in traffic and don't worry about supper." Gerry left for about twenty minutes.

During this time, I started my usual pacing in front of the living room window. (*No one* in this world is a better "pacer" than I am. I refer to myself as a "caged-in lion" when I'm pacing and worrying at the same time.) I thought there really may have been an accident, although we had not heard the EMS go by our house, a very familiar sound where we lived. Strangely enough, I never thought for one moment the boys could have been in an accident.

When I went back to check the food on the stove, Gerry burst though the front door with a policeman behind him. Gerry was crying with his hands over his face. I thought, *I'll bet Dave got a ticket trying to get home in time for supper.* But then why was this policeman in our house and where were the boys?

Gerry spoke ever so gently to me, "Stevie's dead . . . Stevie's dead . . ."

What? Did he say Stevie's dead? Oh no, not my Stevie . . . There must be some mistake! It's just a little boy with a spiked haircut like Stevie's . . . it's not my Stevie.

I consoled Ger with "No, Gerry . . . They have made a mistake . . ."

I put my arms around Gerry, and we all got in the police car. The policeman irritated me because he kept repeating into the microphone, "The mother is coming . . . The mother is coming . . ."

What mother? I'm not the mother! You should be getting the mother of a boy in the accident, and that is not me! It's not my son!

Just then an ambulance screamed by us, heading for the nearest emergency room. I didn't know that Dave was in it.

As we drove up to the scene, I asked Gerry in a bewildered tone, "What is our car doing here?" Gerry cried back to me, very softly, "It is our car . . ."

My dear God in heaven! At this point, my breathing and consciousness must have ceased. My body went completely motionless, and my recollection of the accident scene is completely blank. The policeman told me to wait in the car for what seemed like an eternity. They opened the door at last, and with one policeman on each arm, I stumbled forward in complete silence. No lights glared at me. No sounds blared from the police radios. I seemed to glide over the wet pavement beneath me. The cold temperature did not penetrate my clothing. Even my movements duplicated a slow-speed movie scene.

They walked me over to the silent, calm, peaceful body lying on the pavement. I knelt beside Stephen, picked him up in my arms, and cradled him to my heart. As my face touched his precious face, I whispered in his ear, "It's OK, Stevie. Mommy will take care of you. Jesus will take care of you." After saying these words, I looked up into the face of one of the police officers. His blue eyes brimmed with tears. Then the policemen pulled my arms up, and I gently laid Stevie back on the ground. As his head rested on the pavement, I saw his eyelids close completely.

Later I learned Stevie died at the moment of impact. By the time I got to the accident, he was already dead. This reality did not penetrate my consciousness. As I tried repeatedly to remember each moment with him, I have never believed in my heart that he died before I had this one last chance to say goodbye. Perhaps the Lord permits us these cushioning thoughts to make the burden and shock easier to bear. Whatever the reason, it has always comforted me.

The officers escorted me back to the police car. I gave them no resistance. I don't think I realized as I left Stevie on the pavement where he was going from there. As the car door slammed shut, it crashed through the peaceful presence surrounding me, and the pain of our loss consumed me. Gerry held me in his arms all the way to the hospital, and I cried out over and over again, "My Stephen, my Stephen! I want my Stephen!"

Dave was severely injured in the accident. His left hip had extended six inches out of his body. He smashed his right kneecap, fractured his left kneecap in three places, broke his right ankle, and sustained a skull fracture with a concussion. As we got to the emergency room, the nurses told us not to tell Dave of Stevie's death. They did not think he would survive the night if he knew. Dave had been asking for Steve during the four-hour wait in the emergency room, and to this day we do not know if Dave realized Steve was dead. The nurses told us that they had never had a patient lay so quietly with so much pain for so long a time as Dave had. He did not complain once; his only concern was for Steve.

They allowed us to see him for two one-minute segments during the four-hour wait. I was taken in the room in a wheelchair because I still couldn't stand because of shock. Dave was covered in white gauze. When he saw me, he tried to sit up and asked, "Mom, did you get hurt too?" I took his hand in mine, stroked his fingers, and softly said to him, "No, I'm not hurt. I'm just tired, and they gave me this wheelchair." He asked me how Steve was, and I replied, "He's OK. Stevie's going to be OK."

In my mind this was not a lie. Steve really was OK. He was more than OK. He was already in the mansions of heaven. I couldn't cry with Dave because I wanted him to see that I knew he would be fine. I told him Jesus would watch over him during surgery. As I looked down at him, I saw how vulnerable and frail this spunky, active teenager had become. As he looked up at me, his eyes seemed to beg for comfort, love, strength, and courage.

Dave's surgery was the longest five hours of my life. Pastor Cotter met us at the hospital and stayed with us all night. During surgery, he went out to get us something to eat. I couldn't eat, but he insisted and said we would need the strength. He was right. Two of Dave's friends stayed through the night. One of them came with her mother. As her mother sat beside me, I could see a tear gently caress her cheek through the night. She was crying for Stevie, and she was also aware that we could lose Dave. She was a great comfort to us.

By this time the university had notified Bill, and his friend's parents made the three-hour trip to bring Bill to our hometown hospital. What trauma had filled his soul! He cried and grasped each of us, begging for more time with Steve. "There's so much I wanted to tell him!" What can alleviate your child's agony as he witnesses the death of his brother? Bill was also terrified he would lose Dave.

Many prayers reached heaven that evening and, through them, Dave's surgery was a success. Isn't it ironic that the surgery was "a success"? Hardly a word to describe a tragic accident and the events after it. But he was alive, and for that we were thankful. Although we did not realize it, the doctors did not expect him to walk again. Dave did not know this, and consequently, put his strong-willed spirit to the test and walked with crutches after only three months.

The Friday morning after the surgery, Dave immediately asked us about Steve's condition. Again, I reached for his hand, Gerry by my side and Bill across the bed. I said it very slowly and quietly. "Stevie is in heaven. Stevie is all right; he's in heaven." Dave lifted his head; he looked at us through swollen eyes as that message registered for the first time. "He's dead? He's dead?" Bill tearfully told him that Stevie was indeed dead. As Dave laid his bandaged head down on the pillow, a tear flowed down his face to rest upon the sheet. He just lay there in shock.

How I wanted to ease my children of this terrible pain. How I wanted to spare Bill this moment of having to explain to Dave that they now had only each other as brothers. We just stood beside his bed in intensive care, and I kept patting his hand. Nothing else in the whole world mattered at that moment. All the sounds of the unit fell silent as we tried to grasp the fact that our family would now be only four people. No more laughter from Stevie. No more little brother. At a time like this, no words can describe how you feel. I believe that the Lord's power is felt the strongest when people just stand and listen to the thoughts He uses to comfort them. Then, as we reach out by touching and holding one another, we can relay that strength and comfort to each other.

During the day on Friday, Dave hemorrhaged internally, and we almost lost him again. I think as he digested what we had told him, he began to go into shock, and this in turn affected his condition. God's grace spared him again. Dave came home for Christmas. We were all glad that we could be together, even if the hospital bed had replaced the spot for our Christmas tree.

The Funeral

For anyone who has witnessed the funeral of a child, especially a young child, you can appreciate the sorrow and bonding that is felt as those who come to share their sympathy greet each mourner. Some people say that sending flowers is only a temporary expression and that a monetary gift is more practical. I can only relate how very much it meant for our family to walk into that funeral home and see bouquets everywhere. As we walked beside each one and read the card, the visual outpouring of love symbolized by these flowers strengthened us. It wasn't the size that made the impression, for a number of ribboned single roses were laid on tables and near the casket. It was the message that each one brought. They told us that others mourned the loss of our son, and they wanted to show this by sending one of God's loveliest creations. A creation for the once created—very symbolic.

Many teenage mourners had never witnessed a viewing at the funeral home or even a funeral in the church. After waiting in the bitter cold outside the funeral home and making their way to the front of the viewing room, they didn't know what to do when they finally reached our family. We found ourselves comforting them instead of the other way around. Their presence was enough of an expression for us. They didn't need to say a word, and we found ourselves saying just that very thing many times throughout the day.

What they really needed and what we really needed was a hug, or a touch on the shoulder or arm, or even a smile. These gestures cost nothing and mean so much. When you meet the family after the funeral, don't hesitate to reach out to them with a hug. You don't have to say anything. They will know what you mean, and that physical touch conveys your sincere concern and compassion.

The funeral service was yet another time to reflect on Stephen's life, confront our feelings of grief, and accept his death. Sitting in church with our son's casket in front brings a picture to our memory that it really did happen. There really is a casket with a body, and that body is our child's. We gaze through tear-filled eyes at the serene body, a picture that repeatedly brings to mind the reality of our child's death.

Because Dave was in the hospital, he couldn't come to the viewing and the funeral. A friend of his taped the funeral service. When Dave came home, we watched it together. This was extremely difficult but was necessary to allow Dave to experience the funeral ceremony. It helped him put closure on that period of his life and allowed him to have the memory of the funeral serve as a goodbye to Stephen.

I have not mentioned where our family found the
strength to get through Stephen's death and funeral and
David's operation and recuperation. It is really very simple.
When something tragic happens that is completely out of
your control, when there is absolutely nothing you can do
to mend it, you have just one element in your life upon
which to fall. This one element had been the guide for our
family and individual lives up to this point and would be
stretched to new dimensions from now on. That element is
our faith in Jesus Christ, our Savior.

One pastor based Stephen's funeral service on "I have
called you by name, you are Mine." Another based his burial
on the scripture, "Today, I bring you good tidings of great
joy." That joy was the birth, death, and resurrection of Jesus
so that by faith in Him, our Stephen was welcomed into the
mansions of heaven.

When I first saw our Pastor at the hospital, I grabbed
him by the shirt collar and cried to him, "What have I done
so terrible that my Lord has taken my precious Stephen
from me?" He put his arms around me, looked in my face,
and smiled. When I focused on him, he said, "The angels
in heaven are singing tonight because Stephen has come
home." What glory for Stephen!

Even though I had this thought to hold onto, I did not
cease to grieve for my son. No, quite the contrary. It took
me a long time to accept that a Savior I had loved all my life
had allowed such pain to come upon my family and me.
Even as I questioned His wisdom, I knew that Stephen was
indeed in glory and that Pastor was right! Stephen's death
had challenged my faith.

I have said since then that a parent's faith is really tested
when his or her child dies. Do you believe in heaven? As a
believer, that is where your child is after he dies. If you
digest that fact, time starts to mend this ache in your heart

as well as your body. You will soon realize that the Lord has taken your child to a wonderful place and is taking very good care of him. As John has written:

> . . . I am the resurrection, and the life: he that believeth in me, though he were dead, yet shall he live: And whosoever liveth and believeth in me shall never die. (John 11:25–26 KJV)

This scripture gives us unexplainable joy. A joy in knowing that our child is now in heaven and, although we admittedly doubt that he could be happy away from us, is far happier than he could ever be on earth. We provide our child with the best care and love we can. But in our human nature, realistically, it is flawed, and this is evidenced in our daily lives. Now our child has the "perfect parent" to watch over him. All the care, love, and tenderness given to our child is the very best it can possibly be. He experiences perfect joy, praises God, and waits for our arrival at heaven's gates.

This gives us peace through our tears. When we sit for hours and sojourn down that dark, lonely road of grief, at the end of our moments in pain, we can be comforted by our faith. We hold onto the concept that Christ does indeed have control. He is able not only to take care of our child, because our child was first His child, but He also will walk us through this journey. He will comfort us with His peace and place His tender arms around us, wipe away our tears, and give us a peace within our faith. In John we read:

> And ye now therefore have sorrow: but I will see you again, and your heart will rejoice, and your joy no man taketh from you. (John 16:22 KJV)

God acknowledges our grief. He has experienced the pain of having a Son die. His Son descended into hell and returned the victor over death so that our child would go directly into the mansions prepared for him in heaven. As much as we love Steve, this expression of love is beyond our capability. As we reflect on our faith during this time of sorrow, we have the assurance that Christ rejoices that our loved one is now with Him. This is one of the little ones for whom He suffered and died. He now completes the path to eternal life that He had planned for our child. Life on earth is merely a steppingstone to an even better, more glorious life that extends through eternity. Our life here is a preparation of faith in our Savior, and the prize for our faith is heaven. Christ gives us this precious gift of heaven because He loves us beyond our comprehension. We love within earthly limits and boundaries. We, as parents, feel that we would surely lay down our lives for our children. Not one of us would hesitate to do so. But the love Christ has for our child goes beyond that love and extends its limits to a perfect realm in heaven.

So as we sit and cry, as the tears warm a path down our cheeks, as the pain in our heart cuts our being and strips us of our willingness to go on, we can find comfort in only one perfect peace. The peace of Jesus our Savior.

> Peace I leave with you, my peace I give unto you; not as the world giveth, give I unto you. Let not your heart be troubled, neither let it be afraid. (John 14:27 KJV)

Our Little Christian Soldier

Our dear Heavenly Father,
May we come to You this day
To ask that You watch over
Someone dear who's come Your way.

This special little soldier
Has been faithful, kind, and true
And has pledged his full submission
To whatever he must do.

He's told his friends about You
And has witnessed when You've asked
To move their hearts toward Jesus
And to fulfill his task.

You called him home two years ago
And told him to obey
You said You had a heavenly task
And carried him away.

I know he's serving proudly
In your heavenly honor guard
As he looks up to the Savior
And salutes his God and Lord.

And in Your mercy, Father,
May we raise one special prayer,
That You will give a hug for us
Until we join him there.

Initial Hurdles of Grief

This section is dedicated to some of the immediate issues that confront a bereaved parent. Along with each
one is provided some guidance on how to get over the
hurdles that come before us.

Planning the Funeral

For those of us who have never had to select a casket or
plan a funeral, the whole process can be completely overwhelming. Because of the shock that parents are in following the death of their child, they have no idea what type of
casket they will need or even want. That issue is not normal, everyday conversation. For this reason, it is especially
important that the funeral home chosen has compassionate directors who can provide the extra patience and tenderness that grieving parents require. We were very
fortunate to have someone who not only spoke in a quiet,
sympathetic manner but also seemed to share our grief. He
went out of his way to see that the funeral was as deli-
cately planned as possible, providing the family with the

assurance that all details had been attended to with mini-
mal effort on our part.

The gravestone for your child's grave is also something
that will take you back emotionally. As you decide upon a
stone, which does not need to be done right away, you acknowledge that there indeed was a death. You will place
this piece of granite at the head of a grave that will hold
your child's body. More parents now choose grave markers
with individualized messages and pictures on them. Our
other two sons worked together to draw the front of Steve's
grave marker. This turned out to be good therapy for them
and also gave them an opportunity to have a part in the
funeral. It helped make their brother's death more of a reality to them.

Visiting the Grave

I found it especially hard to visit our son's grave, although I knew that this was a very necessary part of the
grieving process. As I knelt to touch the front of the marker
with my hand, and as my tears fell on the granite, it became evident that my son's name was on this stone. A stone
placed on a piece of land indicates someone has died. Its
quietness whispered in my ear that as definite as the design
was on the marker, that also paralleled the reality of our
son's death.

Putting flowers around the gravestone is one small way
of caring for this life now separated from you. One friend
of mine made a "flower blanket" to place on this ground
before the grass started to grow back. This helped to ease
the barrenness of the coarse dirt covering her son's grave.
Perhaps your cemetery will allow you to place a small tree
or live flowers around your child's grave. Caring for these
plants has helped others move through their grieving and

helps them express their sorrow in a very quiet, loving manner.

Each time we visit our son's grave, it helps us regain our perspective on life. Somehow the cares of this world, the pressures of work, and the disappointments of this life lose their importance. The only care in life that really matters is our faith in Christ and our hope of receiving a crown in heaven.

Support from Others during the Funeral

For those who have a difficult time knowing how to help the family at this time of need, here are some suggestions.

The first and most important thing you can do is pray for the family. Only after you've been on the receiving end of the results of multiple prayers can you truly appreciate the strength, comfort, courage, and hope those prayers can provide. When you see the parents and family, place your hand on their shoulder and give them a hug or a kiss. They are not looking for words but for compassion. No words will ever bring back their child, but knowing that someone shares their sorrow can be the comfort they need.

Flowers are a beautiful way to express your sympathy to the family. Their beauty in the viewing room and at church reminds us of the heavenly garden that our child now walks through. Parents may ask for memorials to be given in the name of the child to a particular scholarship or group with which the child had been associated. This is an excellent way to carry on the memory of the child and also provides an avenue for helping others along the way.

Bringing food to the home of the family is especially helpful. Not a single mother I spoke with felt like cooking and cleaning after her child's death. My son's class brought food for weeks. Although my pride would have normally proved an obstacle, at this time I gratefully accepted their expression of kindness.

Legal Issues

Unfortunately, we did *not* have a very positive encounter with our insurance company. We had no problem with our life insurance but endured numerous confusing encounters from our car insurance. It is very hard for the grieving family to call a customer service representative and explain the circumstances of their child's death. When I called our company, I had to go through five different customer service people before I got answers to my questions. Each person required me to explain the whole accident in detail. This was excruciatingly painful for me. I cried and sobbed but received no compassion or comfort as I desperately tried to relay the circumstances to them.

If you are the parent who calls the insurance company, don't put yourself through what I did. If the first person does not satisfactorily answer your questions, either ask for the supervisor and demand that they speak with you or save the whole conversation for another day. Perhaps ask a trusted friend to make the call as you sit by and provide information. Putting things in perspective, what is so important that you have to put yourself through this additional trauma only to complete an insurance report? There will be another day to do this. Understandably, these reports do need to get done, but not when you are at your weakest point.

Mail Delivery

When our son died, sympathy cards were delivered for months. At first it was hard to read the verses in the cards and the personal messages. But after a while, it became a real comfort knowing that someone cared. Some friends sent cards for months. Many cards were "thinking of you" cards and told us that even though we had not seen them for weeks, we were still in their thoughts and prayers. We even received cards on our son's birthday and the anniversary of his death. This was especially comforting to us.

Occasionally we received mail with our son's name on it. At first I questioned why anyone would send mail to my son now. Didn't they know he was not living anymore? But I had to hold back my anger and accept the fact that although my pain seemed larger than life itself, the rest of the world did not know that our son had died. Life still went on and with it came junk mail and magazines with our son's name on the address label. It was hard to throw away these pieces of mail. I held on to them for weeks. Did I subconsciously think he would return for them? Maybe. Eventually they stopped coming, and now only infrequently do we get a piece with his name on it.

Going through Your Child's Room

Perhaps the hardest hurdle to climb for me as a mother was my initial entry into our son's room after his death. Of course, it was just as he left it. His presence was everywhere . . . on the bed, on the floor, on the walls, in the closet, in the air. Tears poured from my soul as I reached for the belt on his bed, tightly grasped it to my heart, and wailed. My oldest son tried to comfort me saying through his tears, "It will be ok, Mom." My husband told him, "Let Mom cry, Bill." I was crying to God to bring him back, feeling sure that if I cried loud enough and hard enough, God would grant my petition. I cried until I was exhausted, completely exhausted! I lay with my head on his bed and stroked his quilt. Bill left the room after a while, and my husband put his arms around me and held me until the crying stopped. That was all I could bear the first time in his room.

Perhaps you have had a similar experience going into your child's room. The emptiness devours you as you enter, and the pain has no outlet other than warm, endless tears until you are limp and numb.

> The Lord upholds all those who fall and lifts up all who are bowed down. (Ps. 145:14)

It was days before I could bring myself to go back into that room again. But as time went on, I found comfort there. I almost felt as if his spirit was still there. I picked up his jeans jacket and smelled his scent on it, and this just reaffirmed my thoughts. One mother told me that her husband, out of kindness for her, completely redid their son's room before she got home from the hospital. He meant this as a gesture to spare her the anguish of cleaning out his room, but in doing this he robbed her of her last chance to say goodbye to his things. Sometimes the deeds we do out of love are not always what is best and are not always what we want or need.

Many of you may have had similar experiences going through the items in your child's room. There is no timetable with grief. You will read this throughout the book. The same is true for the rearranging of your child's room. My advice is to do it when you are ready. It took months for us to change our son's room around. We did it little by little, first going through boxes in the closet, then clothes, and then moving furniture to other bedrooms and making his room an office to write this book. I knew he would have wanted his clothes to go to some needy family, so we did that. The children were thrilled to get the clothes. As I gave the boxes away (keeping some special items for ourselves), I said quietly to myself, "Steve, this is what you would have wanted." The final step was vacuuming his footsteps out of the carpet. How I wanted to keep them there forever. But he was not coming back to use this room because he had entered a magnificent room in heaven.

> Let not your heart be troubled: ye believe in God, believe also in me. In my Father's house are many mansions: if it were not so, I would have told you. I go to prepare a place for you. And if I go to prepare a place for you, I will come again, and receive you unto Myself; that where I am, there ye may be also. (John 14:1–3 KJV)

We also went through his schoolbooks and posters, his drawings, and all the stories he wrote. We occasionally read this material, and what comfort it gave us. His personality shone through each piece. Perhaps you have mementos from your child. Maybe it's a note or card. Maybe it's a story or drawing that brings you a happy memory and even a smile to your face. I encourage you to preserve these in a memory album. As the days turn to weeks, you will find that you may have forgotten some little moment that you shared with your child, but reading his work may bring that memory back.

Each family deals with the child's room differently. Some may never open the door to their child's room again. Some may save items for future pregnancies; some may share items with brothers and sisters. Parents have to work that out for themselves. As much as I dreaded doing it, and as many times as I had chest pains just walking into his room, when the time came to actually move the furniture, my husband and sons were so supportive that it eased the physical change before me. Grief that was shared during that afternoon became less painful because we all supported and strengthened one another. As we overcame this obstacle, God in

His mercy made us aware of His love. He enveloped us in His care by helping us to reach out to one another.

Your Room of Memories

I strolled into your room today my heart beating with fear,
As into space I gazed to find that you were nowhere near.
I stumbled on your tennis shoes and picked one up to find
That you had gone out of the door and left this one behind.
Your belt was lying on your bed as if you needed it.
You wore it with your uniform; it was a perfect fit.
And, yes, here is your uniform, each crease is pressed just so,
A smaller version of the one that you'd wear as you grow.
Your footprints in the carpet—as I vacuum them away—
Are gently walking on the streets of gold in heaven today.
You had two shirts that were the same, one red and one was white.
You had the red one on that day and wore it on that night.
The white one still has sleeves rolled up and hangs so patiently,
Waiting for you to come back and to wear it so proudly.
I see your Sunday shoes so neatly placed upon the floor.
You wore them to the Christmas program just the night before.
Your pictures drawn from your imagination patch the wall;
They tell the story of your talents and help to recall . . .
Each happy moment you would sit with questions and inquire
Some bit of information from a Dad you so admired.
Your models are so carefully upon your shelves displayed,
Each one was made with special care 'twas more to you than play.
A helicopter model sits awaiting your free time
To come and glue it and to add it to the finished line.
But you will not be able to complete these simple tasks,
For Jesus has called on you and you'll do just as He asks.
Your jeans jacket and gloves and cap can bring me to my knees.
Could it be that the scent of you comes through as these I squeeze?
The hamper has your gym clothes lying on the bottom there,
Along with other clothes you wore—not going anywhere.
And then I look with pierced heart upon your empty bed;
Your special pillow that each night had cradled your sweet head.

The quilt that grandma made for you it witnessed prayers each night
And gently kept you from the cold as I turned out the light.
As I sit down upon your bed and tears swell in my eyes,
I look up through your window, and I see you in the skies.
I hear you saying, "Mom, I don't need earthly things up here,
For I have all I'll ever need without a want or fear.
My room is now a mansion filled with peace and joy and love.
And someday you'll see all this when you reach your home above."
"My son," I answer with a heart anxious for joy unknown,
"My Savior keeps me close to you until I travel home."

Reflections and Roles

The following are excerpts from conversations with individuals who were directly affected by our son's death. As you read each section, you may identify issues, concerns, and similar painful feelings. May it provide some comfort to you knowing that others have gone through this same or similar trauma, and you are not alone in your feelings.

A Dad's Reflection

Living in Fort Wayne and working at Grissom AFB gave me a little over an hour drive home each night. I used this time to unwind at the end of a busy day and to think of family activities for the evening. Looking back on it now, four years after my son's accident, the drive home that Thursday evening was no different than any other trip. Little did I know events had already happened that would change my life forever. When I walked in the door, Jean was surprised to see me, not because she wasn't expecting me, rather she was expecting Dave and Steve. After a short discussion of where the boys were, I changed clothes and told Jean I would look for them.

As I came around the corner, the street was blocked with fire trucks and ambulances. *Must have been a bad accident,* I innocently thought as I pulled the truck off the side of the road. *I don't see our car, so I'll just walk past the fire trucks to see what's going on.* To my horror, I see our car in the middle of the road in a crumbled mess of metal.

Oh no! That's my car. I hope the boys are all right!

I ran up to the first fireman and asked him who was in charge. He directed me to the sheriff's car. As I approached the car, the patrolman rolled down his window and asked if he could help me. I said, "I hope so. That's my car." He told me to please get in the car. After a quick identification check a gentleman in the back seat put his hand on my shoulder and said, "Mr. Werth, I'm very sorry, but your youngest son didn't survive."

"What happened?" I asked.

They didn't know for sure at that point. The man in the back seat, the coroner, said that Steve suffered a traumatic blow to his head and was killed instantly.

"No, this can't be happening. Not my Stevie . . . Not my Stevie," I said over and over.

The shock, the pain, the agony, the anger. Everything whirled around in my head. *OK . . . compartmentalize . . . get yourself together.* I'm a trained fighter pilot. I know how to handle stress and traumatic events. Prioritize and take them one at a time. Where's David? We need to go home and tell Jean. We need to identify the body. But if I don't look—maybe it didn't happen. That can't be my Stevie under that blanket on the ground; it just can't be!

I really didn't have much time to think about how I was going to tell Jean. There's no easy way to say, "Our son is dead." When I got in our house, Jean was sitting at the kitchen table. I wanted to be gentle, but the hard facts came flatly out. Oh, how often I wish I had more time to plan my words, to think about how Jean would take this. I'm convinced there is no easy way to give bad news to a loved one.

The next several days are just a blur. David is in intensive care. But I've got to be strong and think clearly. We've got to make funeral arrangements. I've never done this before. What do you do? I thank God for our wonderful pastor who stood beside us and helped us. I also thank God for a wonderful, kind, and compassionate funeral director who took us step by step and laid out all the arrangements for us.

About a month after Stevie's death, I thought I was ready to go back to work. But for the first time, and for several years thereafter, my one-hour relaxing ride would be no more. Instead of planning my workday activities or relaxing and unwinding, my thoughts are now constantly filled with Stephen, trying desperately to rationalize this tragedy. After four years of going over and over events, I always return to the same conclusion. Our Savior, Jesus Christ, has a greater need for Stephen in heaven. We were the blessed parents who had him on earth for thirteen years.

When I reflect on that idea, all the pleasant memories of Stephen come back. Here was an energetic, enthusiastic boy who had a tremendous impact on our world. I remember all the fun things we did while he was growing up: from playing T-ball to cleaning his first fish; from building a tree fort together to teaching him how to cut grass with a riding lawn mower. My favorite memories, however, are when he would go to work with me one day each summer. Oh how he loved to go to Grissom AFB to look at his dad's A-10 fighter. Most of the other pilots were amazed at his knowledge of the A-10 and were equally amazed at the depth of the questions he would ask, and his questions were endless! On the way home we frequently had philosophical discussions about which was better—Air Force fighters or Army helicopters.

Even though my memories were happy thoughts of Stephen, that one-hour drive was still painful. Happiness quickly turns to loneliness and tears. Initially I would cry all the way to work and all the way home. Fortunately people on both ends of the trip saw the pain and tears and helped me through the day. At work, my good friend, Stu Tobias, could tell as soon as I walked into the office what kind of ride I had coming to work. He would bring me a cup of coffee and sit and talk with me. The other pilots could also tell and would say that I didn't need to fly that day. My wife was waiting for me at home and would hold me in her arms until I could get the words out. Nothing is more important during this grieving process than to have friends who understand and a spouse to whom you can always turn. Over the past four years, when one of us was having a bad day, the other was there to support them. We rarely had bad days at the same time, but I don't think that would have mattered. We realized that we must work at keeping our communication with each other open and honest.

Many of my co-workers asked how I could come to work everyday. I always told them the same thing: my faith in Jesus gave me strength, and knowing that I would see Stephen again in heaven. I can't imagine what I would feel like or how I could cope with the loss of my son without this hope.

For fathers who have lost a child, I would like to offer some suggestions.

1. Keep communicating: talking and listening. Sometimes you will need to talk; other times you may just want to listen. When you talk about your child, convey your feelings about losing that child as well as memories of that

child. One of the biggest fears I had was that I would eventually forget all the things that Steve did or what he was like. If you have that fear, keep bringing it up in conversations or write it down in a "memories" book. After four years, the pain of bringing up Stephen in conversation has decreased, but all the memories of what he did or how he acted are still very much alive.

2. Don't try to be the sole moral support in the family, and don't let your wife or another child take that role either. It would be very easy to close up and shut the world out. I have felt like doing that several times, but soon realized that if Jean, Bill, and Dave did that, we could not go down the road to recovery. At times you will want to grieve alone, but if healing is to take place, you and your family must take turns at the supporting and communicating roles. Jean and I usually did not have bad days simultaneously. But even if we did, we took turns listening and talking.

3. Seek professional help through a good pastoral or family counselor. Whether you as a father think you need it or not, someone in your family does, and it's much easier for everyone if the whole family goes. Initially, I didn't think I needed to talk to a counselor. I am a trained military fighter pilot, and I can compartmentalize all these events and pull them out one at a time to deal with and rationalize. Now years later, I fully appreciate how valuable those sessions were, not only to be supportive to Jean, but also to verbalize my feelings about Steve and what had happened. It may have taken years for me to rationalize by myself what the counselor did in that first year of therapy.

In closing, I would like to emphasize that it is also important for fathers to grieve the loss in their own way. I hope that my experience and suggestions can be of some help to you and realize that it will only be an aid. Each of you will experience and progress through the stages of grief in your own way and at your own pace. You will set your own timetable as far as how long it takes to journey down the grieving path. Your life is now changed completely; it can never be the same. Don't expect it to return to the way it was. Keep alive the happy memories of your child by talking about them. Cling to your faith and the hope that you will see your child again in heaven. These actions will allow you to survive the grieving process and smile again.

My Son upon My Knee
(A Father's Reflection)

I wish that I could put you upon my knee today,
And we could laugh and chuckle as we took time to play.
Or we could do some learning, as together you and I
Discuss your favorite subject, which is "Please teach me to fly."

Your big brown eyes would glisten as each question you would ask,
And you would sit and listen, as I explained each task.
You were my little shadow, each time we were alone,
And I believed your life was an extension of my own.

'Twas easy to show love to you and let you know I cared
For when I came into the house, you always would be there.
We'd spend long hours talking of the things we loved the most;
I'd tell you of the missions flown each day from coast to coast.

We'd plan your future and you'd say, "I want to be like you.
I want to fly and see the world and serve my country true."
We'd also do our chores together in the yard each day.
You'd whistle as you did them, a tune I'd like to replay.

But you are making special tunes for Jesus up above,
And I cannot be near your side and give you all my love.
The tasks that you did for me are now heavenly missions done,
And I will have to do the ones that we did, all alone.

I know that Jesus will enjoy each task completed well
Because your attitude was more than words could ever tell.
You'll show Him all the love and care that you freely gave me,
And when He calls you to His throne and puts you on His knee,

You'll smile at Him so lovingly, your eyes will twinkle bright
And you'll do everything He asks, each one will be done right.
And He will say unto you in His gentle voice each day,
"Your earthly father loves you and has asked Me to relay
This special message to you: 'Even though we are apart,
I love you, precious son. You'll always be within my heart.'"

A Mom's Reflection

Although the first part of this book was difficult to write, the order of events came to mind quickly and easily. Recalling the feelings connected with those events challenged me more as did this section. Perhaps the mother reading this will identify with my feelings and gain comfort in knowing that at some point along our path of grief, we all have similar feelings over the death of our child.

I can't give you an accurate picture of how I lived the first two years after Stephen died. After caring for Dave, I returned to work as a secretary. I had a purpose for continuing my routine because Dave needed me, and I felt the rest of my family did too. When he went back to school, I went to work. Everyone thought I was doing great! They couldn't get over how dedicated I was and how hard I worked in the face of such misery. At work when someone said something about his child, I smiled, but on the inside I was dying. Sometimes I heard a song on the radio at my desk, and my eyes would fill with tears. On some of these occasions, I went to my boss and told him I was going home for the day. He was so understanding. He tipped his head to the side and told me to leave and never pressured me or made me feel guilty. I soon realized that working as I did only masked the pain.

During the second year, after the shock completely wore off, I fell into a state of deep depression. My husband and sons had been so wonderful in consoling me and sitting with me. Sometimes we cried together, and sometimes we sat quietly without an exchange of words. As I withdrew, which was very unusual for me, I found myself plunging into a pit of despair out of which I could not pull myself. I went back to our pastoral counselor and through his therapy, I slowly found a light at the end of the tunnel.

> Come to me, all you who are weary and burdened, and I will give you rest. Take my yoke upon you and learn from me, for I am gentle and humble in heart, and you will find rest for your souls. (Matt. 11:28–29)

No matter how strong your faith is, no matter how much support you have from others, and no matter how much you try to cover up your feelings, a time comes when you must face the inevitable fact that your child is not coming back. That was why I needed to go to the cemetery. It reinforced what I tried to deny, but what I knew in my heart was true. The granite held the name of a child who would not return. If I were to go back and pick one time during the whole grieving process that was the hardest for me, I think I would choose that particular time. But, as is the case with all trials, from that I gained an acceptance of my son's death. I learned what characteristics I display when I'm especially depressed and how to bring myself out of that situation. I'm sure every mother has or will go through this. Some mothers will experience it early and some later, but each one has to acknowledge her tragedy in her own time and in her own way. I feel that I have grown by going through the turmoil and have risen stronger in many ways for it.

> I have told you these things, so that in me you may have
> peace. In this world you will have trouble. But take heart!
> I have overcome the world. (John 16:33)

When I look at myself now and the role I have within my family, I'm sure it is not unlike every other mother. I am placed in a situation to help keep my family together. I try to help my children through a grieving process that provides obstacles, questions, feelings, anger, doubt, and pain that they have never before encountered. I want to be there for them in a way that no one else can. Family members grieve in a way that others cannot. A part of them has died and been stripped away from their life. I felt as if a part of my very soul has been taken to heaven without my consent, knowledge, and in a way that is completely out of my control. The control I had for the years my child lived, a legacy given to me as a result of the birthing process, has now been traumatically lifted from me. Even though I have all these empty feelings inside, I still feel a sense of duty to my family to continue on.

One mother I interviewed has been trying desperately to give her family every ounce of her energy. Sometimes they respond positively; other times she bears the brunt of their anger. Through it all, she has remained a strong, faithful mother and has managed to keep her family together.

The role of the mother with her husband after a child's death also depends heavily on the relationship they had before the loss of their child. An open communication line previously established within the marriage helps to provide the comfort, strength, and encouragement that the marriage partner needs now. Most mothers' tears fall freely as an expression of their pain. Although some mothers struggle with the inability to cry, usually the father has difficulty in this area. The mother can help him by allowing his tears and consoling him in his grief. Sometimes just holding him as he cries will show how vulnerable he is in his sadness, and the compassion she shows can bring them closer together instead of farther apart.

The statistics are staggering for divorce after the death of a child, and I find this extremely sad. Just when you have experienced the worst pain in the world, through a divorce you encounter another loss. Many times this is due to a lack of communication. When both parents grieve alone, this can be a very lonely path to separation. Sharing your feelings can bring about a new awareness of each other and provide a strong bond for your future relationship. As more sorrow comes, and I promise you there will be more sorrow ahead because of the world we live in, you will have this bond, this foundation to help you get through those trying times.

> The Lord is a refuge for the oppressed, a stronghold in times of trouble. Those who know your name will trust in you, for you, Lord, have never forsaken those who seek you. (Ps. 9:9–10)

I would like to reflect upon my personal feelings concerning the loss of my son as it pertains to the relationship I had with him. To tell you that he was the joy of my life would be an understatement. I could easily identify with his constant talking. As a child, I was the same way. Eager to learn, Steve never missed an opportunity to gain some knowledge from the adults in his life. He idolized his brothers and his father. He was especially kind to me but was not a sissy by any means. We were often the brunt of his boyish pranks, but we also saw a twinkle in those big, brown eyes. Because my husband was gone a large portion of the time at his job, and the other boys were at work during off-school hours, Stephen would "take care" of Mom at home. He loved to meet new friends and would always come to me and say, "Mom, I've found a new friend . . . and he's a Christian!"

Stephen had a deep faith in Christ. We evidenced this many times, but one episode is etched permanently in my mind. Steve had a friend who was Jewish. He had asked me a lot of questions about this religion, and I shared my limited knowledge with him in a way that he could understand. One evening as he was getting ready for bed, I heard him crying in his room. This was about two weeks before he died. My husband and I went in, and he was lying on the bed with tears streaming down his cheeks. When I asked him what was wrong, he replied, "Mom, you have to pray for Tommy. I don't think he believes in Jesus, and I'm afraid he won't go to heaven." Steve loved his friends so much that he even cared about their faith.

As Stephen told us this, I noticed an urgency in his voice. Could it be that the Lord had somehow moved Stephen to tell us this before he died, knowing his time left would be very short? This friend never knew that Stephen loved him so and how heavily this weighed on his heart. I know Stephen had no idea of his future, but I can't help but wonder if this happened as a seed for future witnessing efforts. With this in mind, I chose this boy to be one of Stephen's pallbearers, and in so doing he heard the gospel preached with love and tenderness during the funeral service. I felt that this was a last attempt to witness to this friend and that Stephen would have wanted it this way.

What you have said in the dark will be heard in the daylight, and what you have whispered in the ear in the

inner rooms will be proclaimed from the housetops.
(Luke 12:3)

I filled my mind with memories of years past when I
held him in my arms as a baby. How he looked up right
after he was born and smiled at me! I knew this was going
to be a charmer of a little boy! I can still feel the baby-soft
skin of his hands as I gently brought his fingers together to
pray before bed and at mealtime. I also remember Stephen
reaching for the largest strawberry in the container and
smiling up at me as he devoured it.

How he loved to talk at the dinner table! He was always
talking. If he wasn't, there was apt to be something wrong.
I remembered his little hand on my shoulder after a hard
day at work. He'd pat me and smile, and that's all I needed
to gain my perspective again. I recall those rides to and
from school when he sat next to me. I touched his little
knee and said, "Stevie, you are such a joy to me. I'm so glad
God brought you into my life." He bent over and kissed
me. What I wouldn't give for one of those kisses now! But
perhaps he is storing up lots of kisses in heaven for all of us
as we enter eternity.

In all my pain and sorrow, I can truthfully say that I
would rather have had Stephen for a short time than not to
have had him at all. I am especially thankful to our Heavenly Father for this blessing. He could have chosen anyone
to be Stephen's mother, but He chose me. It was because of
no special ability of mine, I can assure you. It was the grace
and mercy of Christ. Each parent is handpicked by God to
bring up and nurture God's most precious blessing—His
children.

The pain of loneliness will always be with me, but as
time goes on, the happy memories provide a wonderful blend
of love and peace. A peace that heals my heart, satisfies my

doubts, and overcomes my sorrow. God's grace and mercy are abundant in my life and shall carry me through to eternity.

> Now we see but a poor reflection; then we shall see face to face. Now I know in part; then I shall know fully, even as I am fully known. (1 Cor. 13:12)

Waiting at the Door
(A Mom's Reflection)

There's not a day that goes by when I don't think of you;
Each hour and each minute precious memories come through.
I see the sparkle in your eyes as they looked up at me,
A mere reflection of the joy that ceases now to be.
I feel the touch of your sweet hand as you so gently placed
It on my shoulder, giving strength and pointing out the grace
That God gives everyone of us as we face each new day,
For you would say "It's OK, Mom! God takes all cares away!"

I hear your footsteps walking anxiously through our front door
And yelling to me, "Mom, I'm home!" It thrilled me to the core.
I can remember many times I'd touch your little knee
As off to school we made the trip—together you and me.
I'd tell you how I loved you and that I was thankful too
For all the joy you've given us and that God gave us you!
For He could have decided to choose someone else for you,
But in His mercy He chose us to walk your short life through.

Did He somehow give you a sense of shortness to your life?
For you lived everyday by seeing joy instead of strife.
You made a friend each place you went and kept them to the end.
You helped them feel special; you had just the perfect blend
Of giving them some comfort when each one was feeling down;
You always tried to make them laugh and turned their lives around.

And yes, I can still see each time, I pause to close my eyes,
Your precious face, and I believe, it's lighting up the skies,
With all the love that you displayed while down on earth below.
The emptiness of your sweet self hurts more than words can show.

I feel as if a part of me has now been stripped away
And that my heart will ever be yearning for that blessed day,
When you will stand at heaven's door with arms outstretched to me
And look upon my tear-filled face, what glory there shall be!
You'll hug me with compassion and in gentle overtone
You'll whisper softly in my ear, "Oh, Mom, I'm glad you're home!"

A Brother's Reflection

When one child in a family dies, brothers and sisters also mourn the death. Attention is focused on the immediate family during the funeral and weeks after, but as time goes on, the other children in the family require their own special care. Each one has a unique pain, but the thoughts will follow some familiar lines.

Maybe the brother will wonder if the parents still love him as they grieve their lost child. They always expressed their love in the past, but now that grief has overtaken them, do they still love the ones with them here on earth? Maybe the child even questions whether the parents would rather have had him die instead of the one who died. Although we can say with certainty that we would not have *any* of our children die, the surviving child may be confused as to his place in the family. Perhaps the brother or sister regrets not spending enough time with the one who is gone. Maybe he wanted to tell that child so many things, and now he misses so much they could have done together. Maybe sibling rivalry had caused moments of disagreement, but now they were starting to enjoy each other when the brother suddenly met his death.

All of these feelings and questions are normal, and the answers can be given without hesitation. But first there has to be a good line of communication between the parents and the surviving children. Encourage them to express their feelings and to be honest with their concerns. Only then can you calm their fears and give them the love and encouragement they so desperately need. Assure them of your support daily. When you see them sitting alone or fighting back a tear, give your children a hug and, if necessary, reinforce your feelings for them. Discuss the relationship the brothers or sisters had, pointing out the wonderful memories you have made as a family. Tell them that you understand their sorrow. Make sure they know that you are available at any time for their conversations. Stress to them that if every member of the family gives support and receives support for every other member, your whole family will heal. As you heal, the lasting memories will brighten your days.

They may be thinking of special times they shared together, such as going to school, playing with a favorite toy, going out to lunch, watching a movie together, or sharing heartfelt conversations in private. As they recall these memories, don't be surprised if the brother or sister doesn't go near that particular place or play with that certain toy for a while. Doing so may prove too painful for them at this time. If the brother tries to live each day with no mention of the deceased child, perhaps that is the only way the sibling can cope. In time, that brother will open his heart to accept his brother's death. You may not see tears, but that doesn't mean they are not shed. Nights can be long for anyone grieving the loss of a child, and for children that may be the time to cry by themselves.

The living children may not go into the empty bedroom for months. Just as it is painful for the parents to enter this room, the children also feel the emptiness around them. As time goes by, this becomes easier. You may find that after the room has been rearranged, the others will go in more frequently.

To help the children deal with their grief, you may want to allow them to have a part in some decisions that arise. They will know that what they think and feel are still very important to the family, and it will promote closeness within the family unit. You may be surprised at how logical and thoughtful they can be at such a time. They may have ideas for activities on the death anniversary, Christmas, etc. that can be very helpful. Perhaps they would like to start their own journal to record their thoughts. They must know that they are loved just as much as before your family suffered their loss and that you can all go through this together. As you reach out to one another, your bond will become stronger. In the future, you will have that foundation upon which to build.

Your children may also talk about the loss of their brother or sister to their friends before they talk to you. They sense your pain and feel that you should not be burdened with their feelings also. Don't be upset by this. Be thankful that they can talk to someone. In time they may turn to you, as long as they know you are available and willing to listen.

A word of caution to parents. It is so easy to overprotect the remaining children. We need to be careful that we do not smother them by hovering over them. They need their independence in the same manner as before. Many of the families I interviewed felt a need to reach out to their children with a stronger hold. During this time, we need to make sure we do not drive our children away. As time goes on, the arms will release and the balance will go back to normal.

Your family can survive this sorrow by open communication, support, and prayer. Our Heavenly Father uses each member as a comfort for the entire family. As we deal with our grief, we have the hope of being reunited as a family in heaven. What a blessed reunion!

My Window Up Above
(A Message to My Brothers)

Although I'm up in heaven now, I'm sure that you must know
How I always looked up to you and that I loved you so.

My friends at school all knew you, although you'd never met.
I talked so much about you and was I proud . . . You bet!

I longed for days to quickly pass so I'd be grown like you
'Cause you did things and went to places that I wanted to.

I liked to tease you when you were up in your room alone;
My antics were just playful, but ones you could not condone.

You'd yell at me and make a mad chase running to the door;
By that time we would laugh and then I'd soon come back for more.

You took the time to come and see the models I would make;
You'd even compliment me on the task I'd undertake.

I smile when thoughts come to mind of our dinnertime each day;
We'd share our cares and happy times and when we went away . . .

We somehow felt lots richer for the conversations shared.
We gave each other time to learn, and this showed that we cared.

I thanked the dear Lord Jesus for giving me this gift
With brothers like the two of you to give my life a lift.

You made me smile, you made me proud, you made me learn to love,
And now I'm waiting for you in my "window up above."

Through it I'll keep on watching you and say a prayer each day
For Jesus is your Savior too and hears the words you pray.

But until I can see your face and laugh with you a while
I'll peek down from my "window" and pass on to you a smile.

So if you look up to the sky and see my face up there,
You'll know how much I love you and just how much I care.

A Friend's Reflection

The number of children and teenagers affected by a child's death is usually greater than an adult's death. Perhaps this is true because when a child dies, the other friends feel as if part of their family has died too. This perception of death affects young people to a greater extent than if someone's older relative has died.

One of the most shocking aspects of a child's death is that this child died so young. Most likely his friends are close to the same age. Persons that young are not supposed to die. They are just beginning to experience life with all its adventure. They are supposed to be on the playground or in the hall at school, laughing with their friends. Perhaps they would be driving to and from school or just sitting in the backyard with friends, sharing a confidence or laughing at a joke. The shock for these friends penetrates their souls. As Christians, they question God's wisdom even though they hold on to the promise of eternal life for the one who has died.

Parents became instrumental as our son's friends learned of his death and worked through the grieving process. The tender, loving way in which parents told their children, no matter what the age, made an impression on the young people. Each one was especially grateful for the parents' sharing of grief and their offer of assistance. In each case, the parents became a channel of communication and support to their children as they reinforced the assurance of God's love for the child who died and for the ones who would now live without him. This legacy of faith turned into a painful reality but at the same time provided direction for God's will for our lives. The gift to every human being is the pathway to heaven and the final achievement— a heavenly crown. As the friends became more focused on this aspect, their acceptance became less painful.

Many have used this event in their lives to help strengthen their faith, concentrate on their goals for the future, and sort out exactly what is important in life and what really means the most to them. Stephen's friend conveyed to me the difficulty he had giving an oral presentation in English class regarding Stephen's death. This friend spoke of how his life was changed not only by the death but also by the effect that our son had on him while he was still alive. These types of assignments have proved very therapeutic to students because they have allowed them to either write or verbalize their grief and share it with others. This, in turn, provides understanding from others and opens up channels of communication between students. Everyone likes to help when someone is feeling sad, and communicating this sadness allows God to use others as instruments of His lovingkindness. We see God in our friends, and we receive His comfort through them.

When young friends go to the funeral home, it is entirely possible that they have never seen a body in a casket before. They still have visions of their friend in school or in the neighborhood. A motionless body is a harsh portrayal of the absence of life. When they see that body, they realize the friend is not coming back. Each friend expressed this in the same way. It is the body, just lying there, that cut through them with the sharpest pain—especially when that body was so full of life just a few days before. At this time friends need each other to hold onto, and parents can use this opportunity to show their children how much they love them by being there for them. It is hard enough for adults to accept the death of a loved one, but young people should never have to witness this by themselves. As we turn to this comfort, we can cling to this passage: "Cast all your anxiety upon him because he cares for you" (1 Pet. 5:7).

One of the items that kept the memory of our son alive to his classmates was his desk at school. The teacher, in her kind wisdom, did not remove the desk immediately but let it sit in the room for almost a month. The students told me that this was a reminder that Stephen sat there and, although he was not coming back to sit in that desk again, it was a small portion of his life that was still with them. The students found comfort in glancing at it throughout the school day. A friend told me that one day he came to school and the desk was gone. Students still looked over in that direction and saw an empty space. This also brought the painful acknowledgment of his absence. The students had to overcome this hurdle, but it was just a step in the grieving process for them.

Students felt the sorrow of not saying goodbye to their friend. Many wished they could have just a minute or two to say goodbye. It is like a door left open and never closed; a conversation begun but never completed. This was evidenced by the number of letters that students slipped into Stevie's casket and sent to our home. Precious, touching letters expressed a loving farewell to Stephen and provided comfort for our family. These letters were so sincerely written and so heartfelt in nature that it was apparent his friends needed to express their feelings.

Parents of a child who died welcome these letters. They let us know that others miss our child. It was especially comforting to witness how deeply these young people were moved by his death. Their words were so eloquent that even an adult would have had a hard time duplicating the honesty and outpouring of love. We kept each one, and I read them from time to time.

Some students still write to us and let us know how they are doing. As we read these letters, we are filled with joy that they take time to remember us. When we see some of the friends who were closest to our son, we are greeted with a hug. How this warms my heart each time I see them. Some even visit our home regularly with news about their future or maybe a remembrance of our son. This also gives us a special feeling inside. As they walk toward the door, I follow behind them, thinking how much Stephen would have grown up by now. A tear always comes to the surface, but their goodbye hugs quickly dissipate the flow and bring a smile as they turn to wave.

All of the friends I talked with had the same ending to their interviews. They all expressed a desire to see our son in heaven and said that they would make the most out of everyday they had to live here on earth. That is a legacy that Stephen would have wanted . . . because he lived everyday as if he had two day's worth of things to do. They also used the word "compassion" as a virtue they learned and would use in living their life for Christ. One particular young person said that he has used Stephen's death as a witnessing tool with his friends as they approach different issues in life and discuss how they can adjust to them.

Telling others of Christ and His divine plan for our lives can help give young people the direction and perspective they need to face the challenges that confront them in the world today.

The Role of Relatives

As the relative of a family that has lost a child, you are in a unique position to renew family ties and express your love and concern for the immediate family. This may be a time to give that long-overdue hug. If words do not come easily, just a touch of the hand or even a smile shows the family that you care. Your support at the time of the death is especially important because you can be of help to the family in a number of ways.

You can coordinate the gifts of food and flowers sent to the home. It is also very helpful if you can intercept some of the phone calls. Talking on the phone and explaining the situation can be extremely draining for the family. It is a relief to have someone else who knows the events relay those messages. You can also help with some of the daily household chores. No family member cares if the dishes are left in the sink for days, or if the wash stacks up to the ceiling. But you could quietly do these tasks for the family. They may not be recognized immediately, but I can assure you that eventually your kindness will be noticed. Running errands for the family, grocery shopping, or handling any unfinished business will help out tremendously. During this time, the last thing on the grieving family's mind is the art of survival. For them, these elements are not at all important, and therefore they are not foremost in their minds. They do, however, need the basic necessities of life to maintain their strength, and any assistance that relatives can give is most welcome.

After the funeral is over and everyone has gone back to their homes and jobs, there is something very comforting about a relative calling and just saying, "How are you doing today?" These calls take only a few minutes. The family may converse only a short time, or maybe they need someone with whom to talk. One of the loneliest times during grieving is when you think others have forgotten. Relatives can shine through at this time and show they care. It also indicates how much they share the grief of the family. Communicating grief by maintaining contact within the relationship helps to bridge the uneasy times when everyone gets together for weddings, reunions, or graduations.

Relatives can help the family by appreciating how hard it is for the grieving members to be at family functions. It doesn't make any difference what they are. In their mind, first and foremost, someone is missing and that someone is their child. Everyone may be having a good time, other cousins may be the topic of conversations with their achievements and awards, but the congratulatory remarks are always mixed with the bittersweet realization that their child will never witness that event or be involved in that function.

During these times, please be prepared for the family to spend some time by themselves. Don't force them to attend these events unless they are completely comfortable doing so. Understand that for some time the grieving family may need to distance themselves. It will not last forever. They just need time to digest the fact that, although they know you miss their child, your life goes on with or without him. As time goes on, they will start to become involved again. When they do, don't forget to show them how much you care by asking how they are doing. Going on and on about your life and getting wrapped up in the details may be interesting to the family, but your meeting may come at a time when they need to know that you are thinking of them. Your support may be just what they need to get through the family get-togethers.

Another way that relatives can show they are keeping the family in their thoughts is to send a short note. This can be just a "thinking of you" note. It can be sent any day of the week. Notes and reminders from friends and relatives are especially meaningful on the birthday of the child, the anniversary of the child's death, Mother's Day, Father's Day, or Christmas. The card shops are starting to make available a line of cards for people who are grieving the loss of a loved one during holidays. I have found these cards to be very touching to receive, and I have sent them to others who have been in our situation.

The Role of Friends

We have never experienced the outpouring of love and support as we did when our Stephen died. Our family is a military family, and our friends on the military base were both supportive and helpful. From the time of the accident, members lined up to volunteer leave time so that my husband could take time off to be with our family. They provided memorials, food, and flowers in amounts that were beyond anything we had ever seen.

The parents and children of our son's school provided so much food that our garage had two long tables full of it for relatives and guests from out of town. One family even offered their home for overnight guests. Their cards, flowers, memorials, and hugs gave us the courage and strength to go on.

These people were used by God to comfort us. Normally pride would not have allowed me to accept this outpouring of love without providing something in return, but I graciously accepted it. During this time you simply cannot repay others for their kindness, and the Lord doesn't expect us to. He has used them for His purpose, and in their hearts, they know that. Perhaps our tear-filled eyes expressing a thank you or a hug were payment enough. Our family will never forget their out-pouring of love. The only way that we can even begin to repay all the kindness is to pass it on to someone else in his time of need.

As friends shower you with their support, you soon realize how vulnerable you are in your grief. You understand and take time to reflect upon a Savior who will comfort you as you flail in your thoughts and emotions. Your minute-to-minute existence is completely reliant on His care. As He provides you with the stamina to go on, you remember, ". . . your strength will equal your days" (Deut. 33:25).

Friends can also make the call or send a card as I have mentioned in the previous section. Many of the same efforts can be duplicated here.

Sometimes it is easier to sit in silence with a dear friend than to converse with a relative. Perhaps the friend did or did not know your son but is very close to you and can experience your pain in a supportive manner. Some of the most memorable evenings we have spent with our friends have been sitting around their table, recalling times when our child did something funny. If they have never witnessed the episode, their initial reaction to our amusing story provides a fresh tone of light-heartedness and warmth within our friendship. The looks of sincerity on their faces show us how much they care about what we are going through.

If you know someone who has experienced the death of a child, perhaps the suggestions in this chapter will help you show your support to the family and also help you work through your grief in the process.

> In the same way, let your light shine before men, that they may see your good deeds and praise your Father in heaven. (Matt. 5:16)

4

Special Occasions and Holidays

Each holiday and special remembrance day throughout the year provides its own challenges for the parents and family of the deceased. In this section, I address these special days and provide you with insight on some of the unexpected developments that can arise with each one.

Christmas

No matter when your child dies, this holiday will hold painful recollections of past years together. Celebrations that held family meals and gift gathering, as well as meaningful conversations and prayer time together, bring those recollections painfully near. As you trim the Christmas tree, be prepared to handle ornaments that were given to or purchased for your child who is not there. Some may find these ornaments too painful to look at and will not want them on the tree. Others will find that they represent a small part of what their child had given to this special celebration and find that gazing at them will bring back happy memories.

What do you do when it comes time to put up the Christmas stockings? Will you decide to hang his in the usual place, or will you leave the space empty? How will you address and sign Christmas cards? Do you write only the remainder of the family? Doesn't it seem as if someone is missing? One less name? One mother gave me a wonderful suggestion. She signs the names of the family members and then in the space for the deceased child, she draws an angel. It's a very simple little figure, but what a message it brings!

The day our son died, we had bought canned goods for a donation at his school for the homeless in our city. Steve wanted to buy "lots and lots" of cans, so we proceeded to fill our grocery bag. When we got home, I put the bag by the back door so that he could take it to school the next day. That evening he died. The bag sat on the floor for weeks before I could bring myself to even look inside. As a family we decided it was still to go to the homeless so we donated it to an organization that fed them each day. Now at Christmas, as we hang Steve's stocking on the mantel, we fill it with a can of vegetables and donate a bag of groceries in his name. Perhaps your family could begin a tradition such as this at Christmas. What a wonderful way to remember your child and help others in Jesus' name!

Gifts under the tree will have nametags for one less person. If your child dies after the Christmas presents are already bought, you are faced with the decision to give the presents away or take them back to the store. We had bought our son a remote control race car for Christmas. In January, my husband and I took it back to the store. I waited outside in the mall and Gerry took it in. The salesman asked why we were returning it. Gerry had to tell him. It was very awkward for him, but this was Gerry's decision. This was just another hurdle toward heaven that we climbed in our grieving process.

As your family sits around the table for the traditional Christmas dinner, everyone is aware that the son (brother) is missing, but no one says anything. This would be an excellent time to offer a special Christmas prayer and interject in its message that all gathered together would like to thank Jesus for taking such good care of the child in heaven. In this way, you not only acknowledge that he is indeed not physically with you, but in a quiet, reassuring way, it helps each member to contribute a small prayer about the child no longer in their midst.

As you walk through the stores, you can be sure that the Christmas carols will also tug at your heartstrings. The seventh grade class sang "Away in a Manger" at Stephen's funeral. This lullaby is played often throughout the Christmas season. Each time we hear it, no matter where we are, we reach for each other's hand. These carols are sad, but they also remind us of why Jesus came into this world and the sacrifice He made for our child now with Him. The third stanza is especially meaningful:

Be near me, Lord Jesus, I ask Thee to stay
Close by me forever and love me, I pray.
Bless all the dear children in Thy tender care
And take us to heaven to live with Thee there.
                    —Lutheran Worship, 1982

The Shepherd Boy Meets Jesus

Christmas is a time of year that brings us lots of joy.
Surprises always come to each good little girl and boy.
We sing the carols of His birth
and raise our praises high
As we take time to look upon
the bright star in the sky.
Was there some little shepherd boy

who knew its meaning then
And what importance it would have,
how brilliant it had been?
And could this little boy have wandered
from his sheep that night
To follow such a star as this, to find a precious sight?
Upon the manger he soon came
with awe and wonderment;
His eyes shone brightly as he echoed
praises with knee bent.
His simple prayer was offered
in sincerest tones of praise,
And Jesus smiled up at him,
as cattle round him grazed.
The little shepherd took his hand
and gently stroked with care
Each little finger that he held, he was so happy there.
But soon the angel came to him and spoke into his ear
That he must now be going, and then she disappeared.
He then got up and went
his way to take care of his sheep,
But angels guarded his return and
then put him to sleep.
He slept not in an earthly bed for he was now above
Where he had many friends to show him
tender care and love.
He knew his Savior when he was down
on the earth below,
And now a heavenly realm was his,
and here his faith would grow.
His family shed their tears for him
and yearned to touch his face,
But they knew he was living under God's eternal grace.
He sees the Savior everyday
and sits beneath his throne,
And we shall do the same with him

when we reach our dear home.
But until then we worship that sweet baby in the night
And use Him as our Guide each day
and Guard throughout the night.
The manger that once held the Babe is
now His throne on high,
And we shall gather round that throne
when we are called up nigh.
So Jesus, hear the prayer we pray to You
in heaven above.
Please keep our little shepherd safe
within Your precious love.

Lent and Easter

The season of Lent is always a time of reflection for the Christian. As we recall the purpose of our Savior's death, we are reminded of our own frailties. Placing guilt upon ourselves for our Savior's death becomes a weight that is hard to bear. When a child dies, family members also place guilt upon themselves for what happened. Whether the child dies from an illness or an accident, everyone can wrench some sort of guilt from this painful event. This process is not only harmful to your acceptance of the death of the child, but creates an obstacle in the grieving process. It may take many years for a person to relieve himself of the guilt.

I sent my boys for gasoline that night. Without that request, the boys would not have had their accident. But when we saw the way the accident happened, the way Dave's side of the car was completely demolished and Steve's side had only a broken windshield, I knew the Lord simply lifted Stephen from this life and that it was meant to be that way. Death occurs because of sin in the world, but our personal guilt should be lifted knowing that God has a plan for our lives. We can't understand it, but we accept it. Sometimes it may involve the death of someone we love. Our healing process is best served by putting the guilt aside, as hard and as long as that may take, and concentrating on the wonderful memories our child has left us.

> "For I know the plans I have for you," declares the Lord, "plans to prosper you and not to harm you, plans to give you hope and a future. Then you will call upon me and come and pray to me, and I will listen to you." (Jer. 29:11–12)

So, when you observe the Lenten season, as you sit in the church pew and sing the songs that commemorate this time of the church year, you may reflect upon the death of our Savior. Because of your fresh grief, you may also become overwhelmed with feelings over your child's death. Though they are different in meaning and purpose, the symptoms of grief are very similar.

As we move on to the Easter season, the mood changes and we are filled with the hope of a blessed reunion in heaven. Easter has given the world a promise of joy at the end of our tears. The scene of the resurrection cross as it is adorned with beautiful Easter lilies gives us only a glimpse of what the heavenly throne must display. The songs we sing are songs of hope and strength. As we sing of Christ's resurrection, and His love for us as He provides us with the same gift of glory, we look deep into our hearts. A tear falls as we sing of those gone before us waiting around that heavenly Easter scene.

Easter is a time when everyone is happy and spring is in the air. A sense of rebirth fills not only the church but also the world. Perhaps we can use this time for comfort as we reflect on the rebirth that our child received when he entered heaven—a rebirth of glory and praise and eternal joy. If we can remember these feelings as we sing our Easter hymns; as we inhale the glorious smell of the Easter lily; as we recall the words of our Lord's resurrection; and as we lift our eyes with humility and awe upon the Easter cross; then we will receive the strength of the Holy Spirit gladdening our hearts and giving us the hope of a reunion in heaven.

"I am the resurrection and the life." (John 11:25)

Easter Trumpets

Today is Easter Sunday, and we celebrate with joy
The glory given unto us as hymns we now employ.
We sing of Jesus going into heaven from the tomb
To take us from this world of sin and from this life of gloom.
The cross is set before us as we worship our dear Lord;
Our feelings are so deep that we need utter ne'er a word.
For Jesus knows the impact that His death has had on us,
Forgiving us our sins and making us all just.
Tell me, Dear Jesus, as we celebrate Your love for us today,
What is it like in heaven . . . can You hear the trumpets play?
Are there some Easter lilies with their fragrance oh so sweet
Placed lovingly around Your throne and scattered at Your feet?
Do children's faces light up as they gaze upon Your throne,
And see Your hand extended as You count each one Your own?
Are angels gathered round You as You look upon them all?
Can You see our dear son with them as he answers to Your call?
What a sight he must be witnessing in majesty divine.
How I long for the day to come when I call that scene mine!
And can You hear each of us as we teary-eyed recall
The Easters past when we could be together one and all?
Please come into our hearts each day and move us toward that end
For You have always been our very sweetest, dearest Friend.
So may we raise the Easter cross as heavenward we gaze

And praise You for the victory as hope for all our days.
Oh, yes, a heavenly Easter brings joy to all below
Until we join our loved ones and can hear
the trumpets blow.

Death Anniversary

The term "death anniversary" was unfamiliar to me before Steve's death. I was aware of remembering the day a person died, but that particular phrase was not a part of my vocabulary, as it is now. As I spoke with other parents, we all had so much in common. One of the events that seemed to bond us together was the observance of the death anniversary.

Some parents started feeling the pangs of the anniversary day with the next month's arrival. For instance, if the child died on the 14th of the month, then the 14th of the next month brought cruel remembrances of what took place one month before. Some parents followed that theme through with the days of the week or even the time of day. All of these recollections produce a yearning to go back to the time just before the tragic parting occurred. These episodes will happen regularly through the first months and maybe even years, but as time goes on, you will sometimes miss the day anniversary or the time anniversary. Suddenly guilt will surface as you feel that you *should have* remembered. But this is not so. It is the body's and mind's way of healing your heart and showing that you have been able to move on to other things in life. You have definitely not forgotten your child; no betrayal has occurred. You have just moved one step closer in your acceptance of the death, and another obstacle has been overcome in the grieving process. The death anniversary will probably always be remembered by the family, as it should be. But the daily calendar will, in time, phase into a softening of only infrequent recollections.

What should a family do on the death anniversary? A number of options will help you and your family to get through the day and days after.

Plan something special for that day. Maybe you could do something that you have all enjoyed as a family in the past. You may want to visit some vacation spot that has always brought laughter and family togetherness. As you enjoy the scenery and the activities, mention something your child loved to do. Others are thinking of him, and just mentioning a happy event will not only take the edge off the day but will warm everyone's heart.

If it is not possible for the family to be together, be sure to call each other. The brothers and sisters away at school who cannot take time off to be with you are also remembering the day. A telephone call will help give the moral support and comfort that each of you needs at this time. Again, mentioning little "gems" of the past will bring some humor to the conversation and help everyone concentrate on the good times together. Then, as each one hangs up the phone, there will be a sense of release. The bonding of grief has occurred, and this communication has provided the family with a closer and deeper understanding of their love and concern for one another.

Something else that will help to lighten the day is to do some type of volunteer work, either as a family or individually. Parents can do something together, or maybe one of the children may want to do something special. Take balloons to the pediatric ward of the hospital that cared for your child, or perhaps take the child of a single parent family to a ballgame or out for an ice cream cone. Volunteering time or taking a few bags of groceries to a soup kitchen or other place that serves meals to the poor will also provide activity for the day. This helps you carry constructive thoughts and benefits someone in the process.

Maybe this would be a good day to go through the clothes that your child had and give some of the items to the poor family of a co-worker or a family at church. At the end of the day, maybe you and your spouse could just walk arm in arm through a park, looking at the beauty around you and talking about the beautiful garden your child is in now.

We have found these suggestions very helpful in getting us through the death anniversary. This is a day when you should not be alone. Sitting in the house and crying for your child may be the one thing that you want to do, but it is not the best thing for you as a bereaved parent. Your child would not want you to cry over him. He would want you to do something on that day, maybe something special, and surely something to help others. Doing that in remembrance of your child helps keep his gentle spirit alive in your heart as well as in the hearts of those around you.

> In this you greatly rejoice, though now for a little while you may have had to suffer grief in all kinds of trials. These have come so that your faith—of greater worth than gold, which perishes even though refined by fire— may be proved genuine and may result in praise, glory and honor when Jesus Christ is revealed. (1 Pet. 1:6–7)

Birthdays

Birthdays are occasions for celebration and joy through the family. Perhaps your family gets together with relatives for each birthday, or maybe you live away from relatives and have always celebrated birthdays with just your immediate family. Whatever the case, they are special days and, as such, have been celebrated with everyone together. Now someone is missing, and you don't quite know how to handle this. As a parent, of course, you are happy for the child who is turning one year older, and you go through the day giving the child with you the best birthday he or she could possibly have. But thoughts invade your mind of the one who is no longer with you, the one who will have no more birthdays. As time goes on, you will be able to hide these thoughts a little easier. You will notice that they will float in and out, take their punches, and then move on.

One of the hardest days for our family is Stephen's birthday. We try to do things much like the ideas I have suggested in the section on the death anniversary. But we have started a tradition that we will continue. Every year on Stephen's birthday we cash in the penny bank that we have kept filled in his room and turn it in for the school's chapel offering. We feel he would have liked this, and it gives us a way to provide a birthday present to further God's kingdom. This offering is then used for mission work.

Perhaps a worthy cause in your area could use a donation in remembrance of your son's or daughter's birthday. The amount does not matter. What matters is the consistency of the donation. It is something that is done especially on that day each year. When I walk in with rolls of coins, our principal knows exactly why we came and where the money is to go. Family members may wish to discuss what they would like to do with a donation, and this could become a tradition. Traditions are an excellent way of expressing your grief and at the same time helping others.

It might also be helpful if other children in the family actually make the donation. Perhaps they could save pennies throughout the year. When the time comes to contribute, each one could play a part in the process. One could make a container, one could drive to the place where the donation is made, and one could hand in the donation. In this manner each one is doing something in remembrance and helping to ease their grief.

> Herein is my Father glorified, that you bear much fruit;
> so shall ye be my disciples. (John 15:8 KJV)

There's Someone in Your Kingdom, Lord

There's someone in Your kingdom, Lord, who came three years ago.
Today he will be seventeen, and we all miss him so.
I'm sure you know this fine young man for he dearly loved You;
I know he'd be next to Your side—do what You want him to.

Are there some other little ones who need a hug or smile?
Why, You could send Stephen to them; he'd stay with them a while.
He'd tell them how You love them, and because You gave Your Son
They now are living in a place that they can call their own.

He'd show them each a mansion with their name above the door;
He'd tell them there has never been Someone Who loves them more.
He'd show them that the lion and the lamb are friends up there . . .
That each one is a gift of God and receives His special care.

He'd mention all the friends he left behind so far away
And say a prayer that each of them will join him too someday.
And if by chance they shed a single tear for those they miss,
I'm sure he'd give each one a hug and on their cheek, a kiss.

Dear Father, You have many angels near to You each day,
And as You look upon each one, Your mercy You display.
For You know how we miss him and that many days are blue,
But You have special work for him within Your kingdom too.

We thank You that You made a special place for him up there
And know that You will give him just the very best of care.

If he ever comes to You, his eyes hiding a tear
For someone whom he misses and who is still down here,

Please tell him that we love him and because Your Word is true,
We know that we will join him for we've put our faith in You.
And until then the memories that time cannot erase
Will carry us through life until we reach that heavenly place.

Father's Day and Mother's Day

For the parents of a lost child, these two days wrench deep into the heart. As the day approaches, dread fills your heart with thoughts of how you will get through them. But this anxiety will camouflage itself throughout the day as your other children give you evidences of their love. They know your thoughts will drift into a sea of memories, and they will try even harder to make the day pleasant for you in return. The Lord has provided their presence to equalize your feelings and help you concentrate on fond memories and the blessing of their being in your life. They are a reason for you to continue on, and just their presence can provide the strength you need.

Moments alone on this day carry your steps down memory lane. You think of your child's gifts on this particular day. Perhaps he colored a picture, drew something, wrote a verse in a card. Quite possibly you shared many hugs with him. This is Mother's Day. This is Father's Day. That's why I'm a father or a mother. Because I have a child. And now that child is gone.

This day is especially hard for parents who have lost their only child. Others celebrate this day with their children, but you have no child with whom to celebrate. You are left hanging, suspended in a sea of despair with no physical means to pull your thoughts together. For these parents, to have lost "all they had" is a most unbearable sadness. Sometimes the child dies after the family can no longer have any more children. Perhaps that child was anticipated for many years and finally came through a miracle—only to be taken before the total expanse of life had been experienced. The only consolation these parents have is the strength of the Lord to fill the void left by their only hope in life. Perhaps a special measure of His love radiates to these parents on days such as these. They do not have the daily activity of other children to lead the channels of the mind into calming thoughts of joy. Their thoughts go deep into painful emptiness and loneliness. It is extremely important that they turn to one another and comfort each other during these days. These holidays will always be days of quiet reflection for all parents but especially painful for parents such as these.

Preparing for the first Father's Day after our son died, I spent days thinking of how I could lessen the blow for my husband. Stephen was very close to him. They did household chores together as well as built a tree house (which ended up being a wonderful family project with the older two boys also) and even played together. Gerry constantly answered questions about military flying for Stephen. I was sure all these memories would bring forth some information for a "letter from Stephen" on Father's Day. Following is the letter I wrote and gave to Gerry on Father's Day. He read it and cried, but he kept it and found that, although it was written by me, it could just as well have been written by Stephen. Perhaps as you read this, you could insert some activities that your family did together and send such a letter on this occasion.

Dear Dad,

Although I am not physically at your side today, my love for you is present in my heart. You are the best dad anyone could ever want.

—Remember when we all got dressed up and played G.I. Joe and all the fun we had in the woods playing army.

—Remember how many questions I asked you about airplanes. Face it, Dad—I knew my planes and helicopters, but all my knowledge came from you!

—Remember all the times we mowed the lawn together. You know my favorite chores were when you and I worked together. We had some great times, and I learned a lot from you.

—Remember that *awesome* tree house. We even got Bill and Dave in on it. Now *that* was a great family project!

—Remember how we swam together, and Mom sat and watched us. You tried to dive like the boys and me. You were funny!

—Remember all the trips to the grocery store when we came home with *lots* of groceries that were not on Mom's list!

—Remember how you taught me how to spit-shine my boots, how you supported me in the Civil Air Patrol, how you cheered for me as a mascot on the JROTC rifle team.

—Remember how much I love you, Dad. You were the best Christian father any son could have.

Today on Father's Day, I hope you will smile with many happy memories of me. Try not to be sad because I am not gone away, only apart from you for a while. You know how much I love you. Keep the memory of my love alive in your

heart. May it light the footprints of your life as you continue your journey to meet me at heaven's door.

Love,

Stevie

Writing a letter like this can help anticipate the day with
a renewed sense of joy, and it can also help the recipient
feel warmth and comfort from those around him.

Weddings and Anniversaries

Weddings are always a time for great joy and best wishes.
Whether you are experiencing the marriage of your son or
daughter or of a relative or friend, it is a time for everyone
to get together. Time is spent talking about family, relaxing
with loved ones, and having a good time. For the family
that has lost a child, however, it also comes with the sharp
reality that the child who is gone will not ever have the
chance to marry or to share his life with someone special.

For Christians, marriage is a special blessing. It gives
two people a chance to express their love publicly and to
live their lives under God's direction with all the joy and
blessings He has intended for those who love Him. As you
sit in the church pew with your mate, your thoughts teeter-
totter between your joy and hope for the life of your child
getting married and to the absence of your other child. Tears
of joy mingle with tears of sorrow. Other children in the
wedding party also remember the child who has passed
away, but in an effort to shield you from their thoughts,
they maintain their sense of composure and reflect the mood
of the occasion with smiles and hugs.

As you approach these days, be prepared to encounter
mixed feelings. A tear shed is always a reflection of love for

someone and, therefore, a common expression of emotion. Walking hand in hand with your mate shares the sadness without speaking words. The clasp of your hands provides the strength that you need to get through the day. A look or smile across the room at the reception lets the other person know that your thoughts are running down the same channels and that you are there for each other. Knowing that you are not alone in your fleeting moments of pain can make the day much more bearable for you and enable you to smile and express your best wishes to your married child.

The day will be a long one for you, but it is a chance for your children to go on with their lives. It is also a bend in the road for you as you travel down yet another highway.

Anniversaries are times when a couple looks back on their married life and recalls the good and the bad, the joy and the pain, and are amazed that they lived through it all. As Christians, we know that God's plan for our lives provided each branch on the tree of our married life. As we recall these moments, our thoughts consistently move toward the memories of the child who is not there. We can use this time to encourage each other and appreciate that through all of this, our marriage remained strong.

The alarming divorce rate for couples who have lost a child indicates how hard two people have to work at their marriage after a child dies. Their love for each other can easily be overcome by quiet grieving, and thus a wall begins to build. At this time communication between couples is most needed. Your future as a couple depends on how you handle your grief in the present. Talking, crying, hugging, and holding each other are outward ways to encourage the other partner that you are always there for him. If you need to talk, you must express that to your partner. Let him know that you had a heart pain during the day that threw you back to the tragic day when you lost your child.

Perhaps your mate had a similar episode during his work hours or on the trip home. Sharing these thoughts brings your grief into one bond between the two of you.

It is also important that you take time out of the grieving process to get away, even for a few hours—take a vacation from grief. When our counselor first suggested this to us, I said I couldn't, possibly because I felt as though I was betraying my child. Then he asked me what kind of child Stephen was. I said he was a happy child who was rarely sad. He said that we should think of how Stephen would want us to be. And the answer was quite evident. He would have wanted us to enjoy ourselves and enjoy life.

Our first attempts at this were clumsy at best. It didn't seem right, somehow, to enjoy ourselves when the shadow of our son's death hung over us. But try as we might to carry the gloom, there were times when we could not help but laugh. At times God's beautiful creation around us captured our sight and thoughts. We had to admit that there still was beauty in the world, and there still were thoughts that brought us joy. It takes time to relax and enjoy the things of this world. Our greatest joy is the prize at the end of our life's journey. But God placed many lovely miracles in our path on earth to creep into our thoughts. We recognize His pleasant visions and enjoy them.

As time went on, we started to set aside a weekend here and there for ourselves. When our son, Dave, was recuperating at home, my brother and his wife came down for a weekend and cared for him. They threw us out of the house, and we spent the weekend at a nearby hotel. What a blessing that was! We were close enough if David needed us, but it gave us some time to relax and get our feelings out in the open. We shared many tearful and comforting moments during that weekend. We even started to work on a memory book with all of Stephen's pictures arranged inside. Their thoughtfulness concerning our need for time alone was a special gift to us, one that helped us gain strength for the weeks to come. Perhaps an anniversary or birthday is a time to get away and have that special weekend. But don't wait for a special occasion. A ride through the country after church on Sunday or an evening ride to watch the sunset provides an opportunity to get away and sit quietly and reflect on God's beauty around us. As you witness His glory, you will be encouraged and strengthened in your walk with Him. As surely as He still creates the beauty around you, He will also create avenues of support and comfort for you.

Praise be to the God and Father of our Lord Jesus Christ, the Father of compassion and the God of all comfort, who comforts us in all our troubles, so that we can comfort those in any trouble with the comfort we ourselves have received from God. For just as the sufferings of Christ flow over into our lives, so also through Christ our comfort overflows. (2 Cor. 1:3–5)

Death of Other Family Members or Friends

The death of a child overshadows any death you will experience thereafter. Sadly, there will be other deaths in your life. You may experience the death of a parent, brother or sister, or maybe even another child.

Fourteen months after our son died, my mother died of cancer. Fourteen months after Mom died, a very dear friend of ours died. The death of my mother, as much as I loved her, did not surpass the grief I held for my son. With her death, however, came the replay of the suffering I initially experienced with our son's death. Making funeral arrangements, ordering flowers, choosing the clothes for the viewing, and ordering the memory folders brought a breathless uneasiness for me. I had three other sisters and one brother to share the responsibility so I was spared carrying out the role of primary organizer. The pain was still there, however. Memories of the funeral we had sadly gone through just fourteen months before vividly flashed in our minds, but Mom's death dealt a blow that to me was somewhat different and secondary to the remembrance of my son's death.

As we sat through the funeral and the minister read her obituary, he mentioned preceding deaths in the family. When he came to Stephen's name, I clutched my sons on my right and left, and the knifelike pain seemed to run through all three of us. My husband, a pallbearer, was unable to sit with us. He did not have this physical expression of comfort as I did. The soloist sang some of the same songs we chose for Stephen's funeral. I hung my head and the tears fell down my face into my lap. I had become quite proficient at crying silently, as I'm sure all new grieving parents have. When it was time to get up from the pew, my sons led me out of the church. Grief had so encompassed me that I could not walk on my own. Family support at this time can be replaced by no other. A parent needs the mate and the children to join the support bond between them. It is important for it shows they all share in the burden of grief.

Going to funerals and standing in lines, seeing the flowers, and expressing sympathy to the grieving family will become a personal challenge for you. When we saw our friend in his uniform in the casket, we were struck with the overwhelming picture of our son as he laid in his small uniform in his casket. Our friend constantly supported our son's memorial scholarship program. At his funeral a fellow airman read the same poem that we handed out at Stephen's funeral. You don't have to look for similarities when you go to a funeral after the death of your child. They grab you and catch you off guard and throw you against a wall so hard that you lose your breath momentarily. Pray for the strength to get through these moments. When they end, you will breathe easier, knowing you have just surmounted another hurdle.

We cannot avoid these times. We have to deal with them. When we decide to go through with them, we should not do it alone. We need each other, and we need to know that God is with us. He does not allow us to go through our pain without also providing the comfort to withstand the grief. God never asks us to go through what He has not gone through Himself. He goes before us to lead us and follows behind to protect and uphold us.

Memories of Mom

The memories come and they linger awhile
And mid all of the tears comes forth a calm smile.
We see her so clearly as she starts each new task
So eager to please us and do as we ask.
One child wants a new dress, so quickly she'd start
To make from some plain cloth a real work of art.
By the sewing machine we would sit filled with awe
As her tender, sweet fingers made without a flaw
A beautiful garment, just glowing with love,
Delivered on earth by an angel above.
And into the night she'd work hard and so long,
And by morning her masterpiece soon would belong
To one of us children, so proud of their treasure,
Given to us with love that you just could not measure.

And other things come forth to brighten our day,
Like her kneading bread on a cold Saturday.
So warm from the oven, each loaf formed just right,
And five eager faces waiting for a bite.

The beautiful pieces that she had crocheted,
Each one is an heirloom, forever will stay
In each of our families in its special spot
So tenderly woven, each stitch is a knot
Of joy and of giving for someone she knew.
Some white, and some pink, and even baby blue.
The hours she sat up with us when we were ill,
Her gentle hand on us, with care gave each pill,
And silently sat and a prayer she would tell
To ask God to heal us and soon make us well.

The remnants she had saved were not put to waste
They formed many quilts filled with elegant taste.
The designs were just perfect, each square looked just so;
The memories like pictures came row after row.
Of all of the memories that can come to mind,
Was her love for her Savior, so precious and kind.
Her white hair would shelter her head as she prayed,
Her worn hands were folded and on Jesus laid
Each of her petitions, both large ones and small,
And anticipating an answer to all,
She kept Him as part of her life 'til the end.
She taught us that He is our Guide and our Friend.
And now she's in heaven with others we love,
Smiling down upon us 'til we join them above.

Following Activities of Your Child's Friends

Following the activities of your child's friends can be rewarding. As you show your interest in them, they can, in turn, give you that capsule of time that you will not have with your child who is gone. You know these events are coming, such as grade school graduation, high school graduation, senior pictures, the starting of the school year, etc. In your mind, you know these things will happen, but somehow that does not ease the pain of their existence.

After our son died, during the next school year our church celebrated the confirmation of his class. One family invited us to dinner. At first I was very apprehensive about going, fearing I would cry at the thought of celebrating this without our own son. But they made it so comfortable for us with their hospitality and warm mannerisms that my husband and I were totally at ease. The son was also a very nice young man and went out of his way to talk with us and draw our attention to light-hearted things in his life. It made the day much more bearable for us, and it was a welcome reprieve to the agonizing hours we would have spent at home thinking of the importance of this day and the absence of this event in our lives.

The high school graduation picture is yet another hurdle for the bereaved parent. As I took Dave for his picture, I was so happy for him. The accomplishments he had made since Stephen's death were insurmountable and yet here he was . . . walking and talking and alive. As he prepared for the picture, I felt such thankfulness to God for allowing him to survive the accident and share his life with us. As I was sitting in the waiting room, my thoughts also fell back on the saddened feeling that I would not be taking Stephen for his senior picture. There would be no yearbook with his name and picture and accomplishments.

As the other students were primping their hair and straightening their clothes, I heard one girl become unusually upset with her mother. The mother, in turn, became irritated with her daughter. I couldn't help but think that each should be thankful that they have arrived at a point in their lives where they can share this important step into the senior year of high school. They obviously had their minds on superficial things. But they cannot be faulted for they probably had no reference point from which to channel their way of thinking into appreciating the little things in life.

As David exited the photo shoot, I looked up at him and said, "How did it go?" He replied with a smile, "Great!" His excitement filled my heart with thankfulness and joy. Perhaps he too was thankful to be doing this. Maybe he even thought about his class picture being the last one of our family. In any case, he made my day much easier to bear and brought a thankful spirit to my heart.

When you witness a high school graduation, as surely somewhere in your life after the death of your child you will be invited to one, your thoughts also will stray to the graduation that was never held. Be prepared for thoughts of sadness, and pray about them before you go. Ask God to help you through the ceremony and celebration, and you will be surprised at the peace He will give you. He knows the pains in a parent's heart, and He can give you a calmness that you could not dare to imagine.

> Ask and it will be given to you; seek and you will find; knock and the door will be opened to you. (Matt. 7:7)

Realistically, again we must face the fact that time goes on. There will be those occasions that bring joy to others but may be mixed with bittersweet feelings for us. At first our sadness is a hard obstacle to overcome, and it is all we can do to attend these functions. Maybe in the beginning, we will have to pass up the invitation and hopefully others will understand. But as time passes, we will become stronger, able to not only attend but also to enjoy the closeness and togetherness that these events supply. When we can do this, we have leaped over another hurdle, perhaps carrying our beloved child in our back pocket, and smile through it all. Enjoying life, or at least trying to find some pleasure or moment of sunshine, is a tribute to our loved one, not a betrayal.

Everyday Reminders

The following section addresses everyday situations that come upon us. They slam us against the wall when we least expect it and cause us to revamp, revitalize, and restructure our thinking in order to carry on with the day. Perhaps you have found yourself in some of these same situations and thought that you were the only grieving person who has ever felt the sting of seeing a familiar picture in your mind that can no longer be.

Going to Church

Why in the world should going to church pose a problem for the person grieving the loss of a child? Isn't this where we should find comfort? Yes, but it also brings a visual memory of the casket in the front of church, of hymns that were sung during the funeral, and of sermon phrases or lessons that cause us to remember our child's funeral as though it happened just the day before.

I have a friend whose son died five years ago, and she still has a hard time going to church. She is a strong

Christian but cannot look at the front of the church without seeing his casket there in her mind. This is a very common issue, and only time can address it properly. After our son died, we went back to church immediately. Somehow we felt that since that was the last place on earth that he was honored, besides the cemetery, that our communion with him and God was still very real. We clutched onto God's presence there. It brought back the sermon and the consolation it provided.

As I sang the songs we had chosen for the service, I remember looking at the cross hanging at the front of church. To this day, as I look at that cross, I am transported back in time to the service for Stephen. This cross gives me the comfort of knowing that Stephen is in heaven. Because of the death on the cross of our Savior and His resurrection, I shall join him there someday. This brings me comfort and should also comfort you. The hymns that we sing on Sunday have a much deeper meaning now than they did before. We always tried to concentrate on their meaning, but because of our treasure in heaven, we now read between the lines and picture heavenly realms of glory to an extent we had not appreciated before.

It is still very hard for me to go to church alone. Because of my husband's job, I often have to do it. Many times a fellow church member will pat my shoulder to say hello, or one of Stephen's friends will come up to greet me. And, of course, there is always Pastor's hug for me at the end of the service. Each time I walk down the aisle that our son's casket was taken down to the tune of "The Hallelujah Chorus," I see that one ray of sunshine that shone through the window on that cold wintry day. The aisle does not engulf me with pain but rather leads me down a path of life that will also end with a ray of sunshine.

Going to church mends the wounds, softens the pain, encourages the mind, warms the spirit, strengthens the soul, and closes the gap between a lonely life here and a reunion in heaven. The more often you go, the easier it gets. Some holidays in the church year will force you to reach a little deeper into your reservoir of faith, but as the service ends, and as you lay your head on your pillow at night, you will have seen the Lord's kindness pull you through and build you up.

> Let us not give up meeting together, as some are in the habit of doing, but let us encourage one another—and all the more as you see the Day approaching. (Heb. 10:25)

Driving in a Car

Whether your child has died in a car accident or at a hospital, I'm sure a trip in your car brings back painful memories. Perhaps your child sat in a certain spot or by a certain window, and now that spot is vacant. Perhaps you held your child tenderly as you made frequent trips to the hospital for an incurable illness. Whatever the frequency or reason, the car almost always holds memories.

The first time I drove our car onto the highway after the boys' accident, I could hardly drive. My hands were sweaty, and I was all over my lane of traffic. As soon as another car came toward me, I gasped, thinking it was going to hit me. After I adjusted to that, I soon realized that the front passenger seat did not have that little person sitting there, talking incessantly in my ear. Steve's absence overwhelmed me.

Driving was something I needed to do, though, and it was indeed a hurdle for me. I felt very vulnerable at the time and easily could have pulled over to the side of the road and sat there. But just as other cars were traveling along the roadway, so I would have to go on traveling the road of life. I could not park along the side of the road forever. Movement forward had to take place, and this was the first step.

When I drive today, I still feel that absence in the front seat, but it doesn't hurt so much. As time passes, the pain will ease for you too. You will make more trips in your car, and more thoughts will focus on the purpose of your errand and less on the vacancy beside you. To ease your mind, before the trip, just look at your child's picture and say, "Come along . . . we've got lots of things to do today." They are always mentally with you in a way that children on earth cannot be. Carry them in your heart, and you'll have that assurance that they are never far from you.

How Many Children Do You Have?

How often have you been asked this question since your child died? Before your answer came without hesitation. You proudly gave an immediate answer. Now, for the first time in your life, this simple question poses a problem. How many children *do* you have? Your answer will be based entirely on your comfort level.

Perhaps you still consider your child part of "your children" on earth and will include him. Perhaps you will answer, "Two on earth and one in heaven." Maybe the circumstances will allow you to explain how you happen to have one less child. Or maybe you are at ease saying one child, or two children, and omitting the child who died.

Sometimes it depends on how familiar you are with the person asking. If it is just an acquaintance, and you don't feel the need to explain, you may give a simple answer. If, on the other hand, it is someone with whom you will have more frequent contact and who would understand your family's situation, you may want to share the loss of your child with them. You can also get your cue from them as to whether they are comfortable asking more details.

In any case, the answer will always leave you with "unfinished business" because they will not be able to appreciate fully the emptiness in your family. But sometimes, if they are aware of it, people tend to show compassion on a level that, as yet, they have been unable to demonstrate to anyone. The situation will dictate the reply, and you will probably change your answers as time moves on.

Does It *Still* Hurt?

"Well, it's been three years. Does it still hurt?" These comments, although well meaning, shoot a sharp arrow into the heart of a parent. Of course it still hurts! That was my child; he is no longer here! It will *always* hurt! Our coping mechanisms become more effective as the years go by, but the pain will always be there in some dimension or another. Maybe not as deep, but its twinge will always be evident.

We have an aunt and uncle who lost a sixteen-year-old daughter to cystic fibrosis over thirty years ago. Since our son died, every time they see us, they get tears in their eyes. They know. They know how quickly those tears can pour out of your heart. People ask, "Does it still hurt?" because they are trying to understand your grief and, as much as you would like to reply as I did, it would serve no useful purpose. We can, however, try to make them understand our grief by telling them that it is a daily struggle that has peaks and valleys and that we are doing our best to move on. Don't be hurt when asked these questions. People will say different things to you and, by their own admission, they are only trying to help. I suggest that you politely inform them that grieving is a slow process, and each person grieves in her own time and in her own way. Perhaps that will put everything into perspective for them.

How Are You?

Has this question pulled you out of your normal greeting and caused you to once again pause before you answer? Being a rather happy, bubbly person, I always used to say, *"Great!"* Now I say, "I'm doing fine. I'm doing OK." For the present time, I'm not great, and it is hard to lie and say that I am. Perhaps you also feel a little less than on top of the world. Giving an honest answer with a smile such as "fine" or "OK" is appropriate and satisfies the question. Every mother I interviewed seemed to mention that this was a hard question to answer. It ordinarily wouldn't be, and in the future it may not be, but for now it is. Feel comfortable with whatever you answer and don't feel as if you have to explain. An understanding person will accept whatever you reply.

Going Back to the Hospital

If your child died in the hospital, or if the hospital was in any way a part of the process under which your child died, you will probably find it very hard to go back there without recalling painful moments. Emergency rooms are especially painful for us. As a volunteer at a local hospital, I only requested that I not get assigned to the emergency room. After the accident, as I drove by the hospital, I concentrated on the care and support we received there. I continue to go there for tests or visits with mixed feelings.

When you go back to the hospital to visit someone, or if you need to have medical work done, be prepared to float through the hallways enveloped in memories of the past. They will temporarily pull you out of reality, but you will also gain strength each time you are confronted with that situation and you pass through it. Just another hurdle you have crossed over. Soon your thoughts will concentrate on the excellent care of a particular nurse or thoughtful doctor or chaplain who helped you with special needs during your time of trauma. These memories will provide you with comfort as time goes on.

Empty Nest

Every parent will someday experience the "empty nest syndrome" when your children leave home for work in other cities, or college, or when they decide that they need to sprout their wings and get a place of their own. This is a normal progression of life and, even though we have mixed feelings about its occurrence, we realize it is inevitable and necessary. Our children need to develop independent, meaningful lives. When this happens as it should, meaning when they reach eighteen or shortly thereafter, we go through a time when just Mom and Dad live in a peaceful house. How we longed for that peace when we had toddlers with an activity level that would challenge even an Olympic athlete! Now the peaceful house, the small loads of laundry, and the empty places at the table are what we thought we wanted and find we have to painfully accept. The quietness screams so loudly that you can hear no other noise.

Our sons were home recently for a wedding, and all the activity that their presence brought with the addition of a new daughter-in-law and grandson made our home alive again. After they left, we returned from the airport. I sat down on the sofa and said sadly to my husband, "Listen . . . listen how quiet it is again." We both just smiled at one another.

This scene has probably happened many times at your home. Just imagine how hard this would be if you were not supposed to be in the empty nest syndrome yet . . . your time was not supposed to come for years. Here you are, relatively young, and faced with an abrupt transition in your life. Other parents your age still shop for school items, buy school clothes, and plan their calendars around the school year activities. Your child is no longer in school. He should be in high school. You should be doing all the things that other parents do, but you are not. You are no longer filling your life with the presence of that special person.

People shopping in department stores, school busses traveling down the road, and groups of parents walking out of school on registration day remind you of what you will not be doing. Not this year, not ever again (for your child). Some parents complain of the expense of sending their children to school. Some parents have a very hard time when children go off to college. Their lives are empty, and they must find something to fill the void. But they can call or write to that child. They can receive cards or even notes from that child. They can still make special things or bake special cookies and send "care packages" to that child to help them feel useful and needed as parents.

But you cannot do those things. You have no one to accept your love gestures because your child is gone. If you have other children, you can transfer your energies to doing all of the things mentioned above for them. But your thoughts during this time will always be complicated and burdened with the absence of your child who died. The "empty nest syndrome" may be a temporary phase for most parents, but in some ways it is a permanent phase for the parents of children who will never visit that nest again.

How can we, as parents, deal with this premature reality? What can we do to keep our minds alert and not dwell on our empty nest? That answer is the same for parents of living children as it is for those of us who have lost a child.

1. If you work outside the home, as many mothers do, your jobs will keep you busy through most of the day. The hardest time for you will be when you come home to an empty house at the end of your workday. Planning a special

supper for you and your husband will fill those moments that would otherwise be long and lonely. Maybe once a week, you could plan an evening out with friends. We have made some new friends since the funeral, and we try to meet once a week for coffee at a local restaurant. We share our day's experiences and sometimes even pour out our hearts to one another. By the end of the evening, we have shared not only a special friendship but received encouragement and honest support from them. Hopefully we have given the same.

2. Getting involved in some volunteer organization can be very rewarding. I suggest something light at first. As much as I would love to volunteer in the pediatric ward of a hospital, and as much as I love children, I am not yet ready to spend my time trying to meet their needs. It is still too easy to transfer my thoughts to comparing them with my son. I can, however, offer my services in other areas of the hospital and thus receive a thank you and a smile that will definitely brighten my day. This also helps to keep me out in society where I can meet people. It is so easy to feel completely comfortable in our own homes after the death of our child. We feel no one really understands our grief, and therefore we need to suffer alone. That is not the case. We will grow in the grieving process only if we have some type of contact with the outside world. Life still goes on. When we are ready to go back into the world with renewed energy, the transition will be much easier for us. I do not infer that quiet grieving is not essential for your healing, but it is important not to become a self-made prisoner in your own home.

3. This is also a perfect time to start caring for yourself physically. Getting into an exercise routine may be more than you want to commit to initially, but you would be amazed at how cleansing a walk outdoors can be. Take even

a few minutes each day, or every other day, to exercise on your own. Exercise videos are available for the beginner all the way to the advanced. Some are only ten minutes long. When you feel as if you are going to climb the walls, doing something to keep your body in shape will give you an outlet for your pent-up energy and push some of that stress and anxiety out of your mind. When you are through, you will be able to take a fresh look at your feelings and cope much better. The exercise will also help you to sleep at night. Grief is always harder to bear when your sleep is interrupted by flashbacks associated with the death of your child. Waking up fresh in the morning gives you that extra energy to do those constructive things you should do and the ability to hold memories of the past without continually falling apart.

4. This is an excellent time for you and your husband to start sharing some of those special times together. Walking around the neighborhood or working on a family project together can fill the evening hours. Maybe you could plan a few more weekends at a favorite hotel or resort or even visit relatives for a brief stay. Perhaps you both like to read, but your schedules have always been too busy. Now is the time to set an evening aside to catch up on that book or magazine. This is also an excellent time to get back into Bible study groups. When the children are young, we are so busy getting them ready for Sunday school and church and helping them memorize their Scripture verses that we sometimes put our spiritual growth on the shelf. Now would be a great time to get involved in a group that requires take-home lessons. You could share as you are doing the lessons, and you'll probably find that many of the lessons learned in grade school will start coming back to you. Simple Bible truths that have sustained you all your life, but ones you may have forgotten, will now come to the surface.

Whatever time in your life you experience the empty nest, use it as a faith-strengthening stage. Use it to God's glory, and you will find that He will bless your family and your faith through those times.

Miracles

Many times during the first weeks, months, and maybe even years, you will sit and cry quietly on your own. You will feel surely everyone has forgotten about you, about your child, and the emptiness in your life. During these times your Heavenly Father can do His greatest work. As you feel the grief pour out of your soul, and as you empty your heart of the saddened feelings locked inside, you will feel a peace come over you that is hard to describe. When you are all cried out, when your mind is clear of all thoughts and memories, when you are completely exhausted, the Lord will put you to rest. You have cried so hard that your energy is gone, and that peacefulness brings a rest for your body and mind.

I always felt that Jesus took His hand, put it over my eyes, and said in a calm, soothing voice, "You have cried enough . . . now it is time to rest." I often slept in the chair for half an hour or more. When I woke up, I felt renewed and encouraged. I knew the situation in my life had not changed, but I discovered one very important thing. I got through a deep despairing moment, and with the Lord's help, I'm going to go on. This is especially meaningful to the parent or friend who feels there is nothing left for which to live. My child or my best friend is gone, and I don't know how to go on. As you allow Jesus to lead you through these valleys of sorrow and despair, you will soon come to rely on Him more and more to guide your life. Your faith will strengthen, and you will have the assurance that He will always be with you. You are not grieving alone, not now, not ever. I am reminded of the scripture:

> Are not two sparrows sold for a penny? Yet not one of them will fall to the ground apart from the will of your Father. And even the very hairs of your head are all numbered. So don't be afraid; you are worth more than many sparrows. (Matt. 10:29–31)

At times you will be home alone. Your other children are at school, and your husband or wife is at work. The shadow of your child's death may start to consume your thoughts, and you may feel very uneasy and anxious. Perhaps this would be a good time to call a close friend, someone who understands your sorrow. Always ready to accept a phone call, your pastor or counselor is there to encourage and uplift you. You don't need to grieve on your own unless you feel that this should be a solitary time for you. There are always people to comfort you. The biggest obstacle that you have to overcome is to put your pride in your pocket and accept their offers of help. We have many friends who are hurt if we *don't* call them. They are so willing to help, and they insist that they want to be there for us. Maybe it's just to listen or to hold your hand. It gives them an opportunity to help you through your grief and helps them at the same time. If you are fortunate enough to have friends like this, and you can be assured that your Heavenly Father placed them in your life as instruments of His lovingkindness, please accept their gifts of time.

Christian Radio

We live in an area of the United States that has two Christian radio stations. Christian radio stations are located throughout the U.S., but not all cities are fortunate enough to have one, so this service may not be available to everyone.

If there is a station in your area, I strongly encourage you to listen to it daily. After our son died, I heard the song "Peace Be Still" on our local station. Al Denson sang it, and the words were exactly what we needed to hear. It spoke to us in such a way that we could envision our Savior telling us those very words. We bought the cassette and played it over and over. Each time we heard it, whether at home or on the radio, we cried. But the tears were cleansing tears. When the song ended, we sighed and went on with what we were doing. Perhaps a special song has touched your heart since the death of your child or friend. As we listen everyday, we are encouraged by Scripture, beautiful songs, and informative segments that help us to gain greater insight into our faith and our everyday life.

These stations also provide avenues for listeners to use signs of remembrance for their child. Sponsoring a time slot or a day in memory of your child can help you symbolize the significance of the day your child entered heaven. You will be surprised at the feedback you will receive from others as they too listen to that particular station. The songs played on one station in our area during our day of sponsorship dealt with the Christian family. Even though they brought tears to our eyes, they comforted us. The Lord can use this avenue of ministry to remind us of His goodness and grace even when we are driving, cleaning, eating, or just relaxing. And what better music to have our families listen to than music of God's love!

Going Back to Work

After the death of your child, you will eventually go back to work. Daily duties that were second nature to you before will require more concentration at first. It will be a little harder to keep your mind on what you are doing. Your thoughts will often stray to the time you spent home after your child's death. But as time goes on, you will feel more comfortable with your work surroundings.

During this time an understanding employer and co-workers can provide a support base for you. Maybe they will ask, "How are you really doing today?" The answer need not entail a dissertation on your feelings, but if they were not concerned, they would not ask. Their confidence in you and your ability can give you the needed strength to get through the day. Most likely some co-workers may make absent-minded remarks, but do not let them get you down. These people have not gone through what you have, and your meekness and sustaining spirit will in the end speak louder about your Christian attitude than correcting their rude remarks. Your compassion toward others and your acceptance of their attitude toward you will be an example to everyone with whom you work. Pray for strength to get through the day, and doing your best will come by God's mercy. If there are some days or moments when you need to leave your desk or take a vacation day, allow yourself the luxury. Your past work ethic will dictate your loyalty through these times.

Daily Visions

How blessed you are that you can step
into your plane each day
And soar way up beyond the clouds
from earthly problems stray.
The energy you use to thrust your plane into the air
Is only challenged by the skill
that you display with care.
As up into the heavens, you embrace each puffy cloud,
The solitude and peacefulness
around you does enshroud.
But do you often wonder as you touch the sky of blue,

If Jesus holds a message there
that's meant for only you?
Can He be whisp'ring in your ear, in gentle overtones
That you are near to those you love,
and whom He has called home?
Are there some precious silhouettes
that smile into your face,
And do the features gently touch your heart
from this vast space?
Can you hear someone calling you
and giving you a glow
Of warmth and love that can't be felt by
those on earth below?
I'm sure you say a prayer as heavenly beauty you enjoy
And wish that each one of us could
your time in flight employ.
And as you land your aircraft
and then turn your engines down,
You wait for yet another chance to glimpse
God's holy crown.
Written for my husband

Family Photographs

What do you do when someone wants a family photograph? Everyone is gathered for a reunion or a family celebration. Someone shouts, "It's time for family pictures!" Haven't we all been in this situation? Everyone gets out his camera, and flashbulbs go off everywhere. Everyone smiles and stands straight. On the surface it appears that this is a happy moment for everyone involved. They will not remember that when it comes to your family picture, it will never be complete again. There will be someone missing. But you still smile and go on with the routine. When the pictures are developed and you look them over, you smile at your spouse and whisper, "It's a nice picture, but it would be better if all of us were there."

It's time for your church to take family pictures for the directory. This is an especially hard time because other families are having their pictures taken before and after yours. Perhaps some of these families have children the same age as your child would have been. You sit in the waiting room, glancing at these other families. Of course, you maintain that same smile, but inside you are crying, wishing your whole family could also be there. When the book is printed, they never include the name of the child who is gone. They list only the names of the family members in the picture. Looking through the directory pierces your heart because it reminds you again that your child is not an earthly member of your family any longer. But be consoled that your child is a member of a much larger family—the family of believers who have reached their heavenly home. He is pictured with the Creator of all beautiful pictures and families of this world.

Mealtime

Mealtime at our house took on various stages after our son's death. At first we didn't eat at the table. Our son, David, lay in a hospital bed in the family room, so we took his food in there and ate with him. This was a very convenient way to avoid sitting at the kitchen table and face the inevitable awkwardness there. After David could use a wheelchair, we slowly starting putting things on the table and eating buffet style, going to the table but not really eating there yet. This went on for a few weeks and worked out fine.

After three months, David went back to school. When he came home at the end of the day, he put down his crutches and sat at the table to talk before supper. Now we were faced with eating at this table because we were all there anyway. For parents who have lost children, it is very hard to sit around that table and not set a place for the child missing. His absence creates such an open space. A real person used to sit there. He ate and laughed and talked and prayed together with everyone else. Now that space is empty. You start your meal by praying, and everyone notices one less voice. At least we had David's voice for a while, but when he left for college, it was so sad to hear only two voices praying before meals.

Let's not forget that we have to adjust how much food we make, especially if that child was a good eater. Those extra portions are no longer necessary. We may still make way too much spaghetti or casserole or too many potatoes for the meal at night. Our milk consumption will go way down, and cereal will last a lot longer. What we would give to buy an extra carton of milk or an extra box of cereal now.

Then there are only three plates at the table. Or maybe only two. The table seems to be so much larger now. There is more than enough room for anything you can put on it. There is plenty of leg room; plenty of room for elbows; plenty of room for cups, silverware, and napkins; plenty of lulls in the conversation for laughter and recalls of daily activities. All this extra room just accents the obvious. Reality has once again set in.

In our prayers, we pray that Jesus is the unseen guest at every meal. We feel His presence even though we cannot see Him. By the same token, our child's memories are with us and form an unseen presence for us also. The comforting aspect of this is that our child and Jesus now share a heavenly feast that we can only dream about.

How lovely is your dwelling place, O Lord Almighty!
My soul yearns, even faints, for the courts of the Lord;
my heart and my flesh cry out for the living God. Even

the sparrow has found a home, and the swallow a nest for herself, where she may have her young—a place near your altar, O Lord Almighty, my King and my God. Blessed are those who dwell in your house; they are ever praising you. (Ps. 84:1–4)

Child's Death Due to a Car Accident

More children die each year due to car accidents than any other cause of death. No matter how your child or your friend dies, it is going to be painful. When a child dies from an extended illness, the survivors have a special time of grace to prepare somewhat for the end. This may be a positive or a negative burden. It is positive because it alerts your body and mind to the inevitable, and you begin to mourn even though you don't really realize it. When your child dies, the end is devastating, but you could slowly see it coming as you journeyed down the dreadful road of despair. On the other hand, watching your child suffer for days, months, or even years can require a patience that is only given through your Heavenly Father. At this time He will sustain you and "bear you up" as you prepare for the end.

When your child dies in a car accident, however, you are not given a chance to prepare for the loss. You are not given a chance to say goodbye or to give that last hug to a failing little body. Perhaps you are able, as was our case, to go to the scene and hold that child in your arms, but there will be no response. That child will have already arrived in heaven. You are saying, "See you in a little while" on earth and have no idea that the phrase you utter so casually will be the invitation consuming your thoughts for the rest of your life. "See you in a little while" is what you cling to as you grieve the loss of your child. Perhaps this unfinished business makes the accidental death so frustrating, opening the road to guilt for the parent. In our society, it seems that things are always hovering in our minds if they are left unfinished. It takes a long time to accept that this child was "handpicked" by God on that day, and that the act itself did not require or need your permission. It just happened.

It is necessary at this point to provide some input and encouragement for the person driving the car that held the child who died.

The first chapter of this book brought you into the intensive care unit as we told our son, David, that his brother was in heaven. You saw a picture of extreme sorrow, pain, and disbelief on the part of our son. As long as I live, I will never forget the look on his face. I interviewed a mother who was driving the car when her son was killed in an auto accident. This woman is extremely strong and courageous, a woman to be admired for her steadfast faith and ability to go on with her life. She offers insight on survival and release from the guilt of the accident to others who have found themselves plunged into the same situation.

I asked, "As a mother and driver of the vehicle, what have you done to deal with the death of your son?"

She replied, "I have consoled myself by concentrating on three areas:

1. I have learned of other accidents where a family member was driving the car and a family member had died. I have looked to these survivors, and that has given me the courage to go on.

2. Our family has had professional counseling, and that has helped us to deal with the circumstances surrounding our son's death.

3. I know that all drivers make driving errors. Each error is wrong, but one is no more wrong than another. Something a driver has done may have been an error and caused an accident, but the driver did not cause a person's death."

As the interview continued, we also discussed what advice she would give others in her position. She stated, "I would tell the older person to rely on their reservoir of faith to get him through. A younger person may not have that reservoir, so it will be harder for him. And I'd tell all that Jesus can forgive anyone and to concentrate on that for their strength."

> Fear not little flock; for it is your Father's good pleasure to give you the kingdom. (Luke 12:32 KJV)

As the family concentrates and focuses on this scripture, we are given a peace that helps us to accept whatever has happened. This peace can bring our family closer together because we will be aware that it is only through the grace and love of God that our child has been called to heaven, and it is that same grace and love that will carry us there.

For family members who were not driving the vehicle during the accident, it presents a challenge to you to accept the accident and how it happened. We are reminded of the Bible passage:

> No temptation has seized you except what is common to man. And God is faithful; he will not let you be tempted beyond what you can bear. But when you are tempted, he will also provide a way out so that you can stand up under it. (1 Cor. 10:13)

This gives us, as well as the driver of the vehicle, comfort. It states very simply that God has control of our lives. It tells us that no matter what comes our way, God will provide that avenue to not only get through a situation but also be able to bear it through His strength. He knows before we are born how long we will live and when He will call us to the mansions of heaven. That does not mean that we need to take reckless chances with our lives, but it does provide a clear picture that all our lives are under His control. The knowledge and power of His almighty hand will determine what passes through our lives and how long our lives pass through this world. Because He knows how painful it is to have a son die, He knows the pain we endure.

Because of His experience and His grace, God will help all family members and friends to walk down the path of grief and sorrow. Although we may believe that we have total control over our actions, we know that God has the ultimate control in our lives. When we are involved in an event that takes another person's life, we are reminded that God Himself has chosen to receive that person into heaven at that particular moment. The results of that child's death on earth may not even be evidenced immediately. But we have the assurance that God does all things for our good. That may seem like a rather calloused remark coming from a parent who has lost a child, but if you think about it, it is true. The good that came out of the loss of your child is that your child has been received into heaven.

One of the students I interviewed said it with great conviction. "Stephen is now in a place that we long to be someday. He is in the most enviable place, a place that we can look forward to going." That was quite succinct a point for a young man to make, but it is true. Although our child's death hurt us terribly, we know that Stephen has received the crown that all believers will someday receive—a crown of glory praising the Father Who loves him even more than we do, as hesitant as we may be to admit it. The Heavenly Father Who made him has now called him home. The driver of the vehicle was only an instrument of God's will. Because he or she was an instrument, God will give that person and that family an extra measure of His comfort, grace, and mercy to deal with the death and the vision to experience a blessed and joyful reunion in heaven someday.

Going down the street where the accident occurred can be like a knife cutting through your heart. Each time we pass the street where the accident took place, I look down to the spot where our son died. It is very hard for me to drive down that street. I will take an alternate, longer route to get home. My husband and my sons accommodate my request to do the same if I am in the car. If, however, the accident occurred on a street that you must drive each day, you are constantly confronted with the memory. As time goes on, the flashback will stay for a shorter time on your journey. If someone else is in the car, your conversations will keep your mind going in a specific direction, and that will help alleviate the pain.

Special Reminders

As you drive, do you now have a new awareness of the creation of God around you? When we took a trip to West Point last summer, one little bird hovered over our car for about half an hour. As I looked up, I remembered that if the Lord watches over that lone bird on this busy thoroughfare, surely He cares for our child in heaven. Shortly after the accident, I drove down a country road. Suddenly I looked off to my left and saw a young fawn all by itself in a field. It was just about to run across the road. As I got closer, it stopped and looked right at me. It stood safely in the field without crossing the road. This indicated to me that the Lord cares for even his smallest creatures and therefore has a special place for our son in His kingdom.

My favorite time is sitting on the sofa in our family room and watching a robin's nest in the tree just outside our window. This robin and her nest have provided such symbolism to me that I could not forget its impact. No matter how hard the wind blew, no matter how much ice gathered on the branch, no matter how bad the blizzards bent the branches, that nest stayed securely fastened to the joint of the branches. In the summer when the rains and lightening twisted the leaves and tore away at the nest, the mother robin stayed with her young.

Was the Lord showing me a valuable lesson with this robin in its nest? Could the nest be the foundation of His Word, giving us strength, shelter, and comfort during trials and tribulation? The robin symbolizes our Heavenly Father. No matter what elements come against our lives, He will not leave us. He will hold on to protect us. We are the little babies in the nest, vulnerable and weak in our grief. He knows this and cares for us. Although we will go through days of sorrow and doubt, asking questions as to why and why me, answers come only from Him in His time. The answers may not be evident right away; they may not be evident while we are here on earth, but we are assured that they will be answered in heaven.

When you drive down the street, do you notice other children who would be your child's age playing in the yard or perhaps riding a bike exactly like the one your child rode? Perhaps a child with a similar cap or jeans jacket brings back memories to you. As you continue to pass these reminders, you eventually smile because their presence brings back happy memories instead of sad ones. You find yourself concentrating on a time that will never be recaptured. For just that instant, however, it gave you a glimpse of your whole family, a time when a normal daily routine filled your life. Although these total family pictures in your mind can never again be, just the remembrances of them can lighten your day and bring a smile to your heart.

Avenues for Healing

As you experience your new life without your child, you will also look to the future. This projection into the unknown will not come right away. You may not even want to think of a future without your child, but it will always be there in front of you, and you will live everyday in it whether you want to or not. You can take a variety of measures to keep positive thoughts before you and give you the energy to get through not only today but also the years ahead.

Professional Counseling

The first step that is helpful to any family losing a child, and even for friends of the deceased, would be to seek some sort of professional counseling. Marriage and family therapists also deal with grief counseling. The counselor we chose was referred to us by our pastor. As insightful as your clergy may be, they may not be trained to deal with problems involving the death of a child, especially if that death is complicated by the involvement of another family member.

Professional counseling can provide an avenue of healing that you may have reached on your own, but much farther down the road, or in some cases, may not have reached at all.

We found the guidance of our Christian counselor very helpful. We also felt that receiving his therapy gave us the opportunity to communicate our grief to one another in a way that did not threaten us. The setting allowed us to say things that we would have found very difficult to say to one another in our home. Somehow answering his questions brought out the sad feelings that were hidden in the confines of our home. As we revealed those feelings, other family members received a greater appreciation of what each one was going through. Each session had definite Christian overtones, which also gave us the comfort and encouragement we needed. For anyone who is going through this same loss, counseling would be very beneficial.

I'd like to address the role of counseling for a family who has experienced a miscarriage or stillbirth. Each day a large number of families experience that type of loss. Those with miscarriages suffer in silence because there is no funeral or outward expression of grief that comes with a birthed child. The families that were interviewed who had one or even multiple miscarriages were very sincere in their expression of pain and hurt. They know that this was a real child, no matter how small it was in the womb. The Lord has a special place for these little ones, and the questions surrounding their absence from our lives can only be answered in heaven. Sadly, very few of these couples receive counseling for themselves or their families. One pastor stated that he had counseled only one case of miscarriage loss in his many years of ministry. Perhaps this is because women go back to work soon and go on with their daily activities. The women I interviewed may have gone back to work, but their pain was still very real to them throughout their day. They gained comfort by others showing care and concern. Those parents always remember when they had that miscarriage and wonder about their child in heaven's cradle.

For those parents who have waited a long time to have a child, only to have it end in a stillbirth or a death shortly after birth, counseling may provide a means whereby they may vent their grief and bring the family closer together as they grieve for the child. Again, there will be questions, but where questions rise, faith will fill the gaps.

A spot in a nearby cemetery has been set aside as Babyland where stillbirth and young children are buried. Those who visit the gravesite can see all the other families who have gone through this similar situation. What a comfort to know that you are not alone in what you are going through. This, in some small way, helps us to endure. Perhaps God can use someone who has gone through this to comfort you as you struggle down the path for the first time alone.

> Praise be to the God and Father of our Lord Jesus Christ, the Father of compassion and the God of all comfort, who comforts us in all our troubles, so that we can comfort those in any trouble with the comfort we ourselves have received from God. For just as the sufferings of Christ flow over into our lives, so also through Christ our comfort overflows. (2 Cor. 1:3–5)

Along with counseling, other things can help you when you are feeling blue and desperately trying to maintain some sort of sanity about your grief. Keeping your lights on in the house, pulling the curtains open, and playing some uplifting Christian music can help to brighten your day.

Somehow when the sun shines, we are better able to cope with almost anything. As you look out on a sunny day, you can envision thoughts of your child playing or doing something funny in the yard. I'm sure as these thoughts cross your mind, a smile will quickly come.

My last piece of advice would be to pray with a friend or bring your hands together in prayer by yourself. The power of God's love can only be experienced as we reach the depths of despair and reach out to Him. He works His majestic powers when we are completely dependent on Him. What comfort and tenderness He will give you as you lay your heart and soul upon Him.

> Cast all your anxiety on Him because he cares for you.
> (1 Pet. 5:7)

Communication with One Another

As you experience the loss of your child, or in some cases your friend, you will feel the temptation to grieve all by yourself. While solitary moments are gratifying and even helpful, it is not a healthy routine for your forward movement in the grieving process. Communicating with others provides the expression and thereby acknowledgment of grief. Conversing with someone allows you to express words that you may have had difficulty accepting. Phrases such as "my child died" or "my child is gone" can be tucked safely away in the crevices of your mind, but once they are spoken, they are a reality. They acknowledge that this act did indeed happen. It has been years since our son died, and I still have trouble saying, "My child is dead." I can say, "He died in a car accident," but to say he is dead is still rather gripping for me. In time I know this too will get easier to say.

Conversation between husband and wife is essential for the acceptance of grief and for the health of the marriage. As your children hear you talk about your feelings and memories, it helps them to contribute to the conversation. You get an idea of where they are in the grieving process, and each family member will strengthen the other person and thereby gain strength too. Sharing your faith at this time also puts the death into a Christian perspective that, until stated, may have become overshadowed by doubt and anger. Young family members or friends may need adults to clarify God's plan for all our lives in order to adjust their feelings. Adults will not have all the answers, but their conviction and truthfulness show young people how to incorporate their faith during times such as these. They will remember this example as they cross other highways throughout their lives. It will also assure them of the parents' role of support and compassion so desperately needed in our society today.

Young people can also support the parents during this time. Many days I came home from work and walked up the stairs crying only to find my son ready to extend his arms of comfort to me. What compassion he showed at such a young age! Sometimes a TV show came on with a young actor about our deceased son's age. The thought of what might have been overwhelmed me, and the tears began to flow. At these times David came over and wrapped his arm around me. His shoulder held my weary head, and his compassion filled my heart. Although I felt that I should be the strong one for my family, I soon learned that the Lord used even my recuperating son to express the lovingkindness that He meant for our family. The focus here is that family members can work together to comfort each other just by showing affection and keeping communication open.

Time for Yourself

Moms have written that they were in a state of shock for years after the death of their child. This stage in the grieving process took many different forms. Some mothers could not function outside the home. They simply stayed indoors and did very little during the day but grieve. Some mothers returned to work in time, but as the work schedule drained them of all their energy, they returned home at night feeling completely overwhelmed and exhausted. Making a meal for their family was too much to even think about much less prepare.

Friends can help during these times. Perhaps someone will call and offer to bring over that extra casserole made during the day. They may even invite your family over for a quick supper. Eating out occasionally can slowly bring you outside the house and at the same time allow your family to share the day's experiences over a meal without the pressure of preparation and cleanup.

Housekeeping may require too much energy for the grieving parent. Even if members of the family pitch in to do chores, those corners and crevices still require a thorough cleaning. Perhaps you can afford a cleaning service for those tasks. We found this very helpful after our son died. When I came home from work, I was exhausted. Just coming into a clean house helped me feel better. If someone wants to help your family after the initial mourning period is over, this would be an excellent way. Eventually you will get back to the housekeeping chores, but for a while it is a nice treat and allows you to save your energy, pacing yourself along the way to healing.

Outward Expressions

There are a number of ways to work through your grief in a physical manner. I have listed only a few, but I'm sure you could think of many others. Perhaps you are doing just that.

As the eighth grade graduation came closer, we dreaded the thought of how to cope with the fact that Stephen's class was not only a year older but was moving on to another milestone, namely high school. During the graduation ceremony, the coordinator played a video for the class. The video showed our son marching at the basketball game and twirling his rifle. After the video, my husband and I stepped to the podium. As I looked into the audience, my heart was deeply touched by the tears on the faces of not only the children but also their parents. As hard as it was, I read a speech I had written about the importance of a Christian relationship between parents and children. I stressed that children are a blessing from the Lord and that parents have a duty to provide the best environment possible for them. I also expressed to the students that the Lord has chosen very special people to be their parents, and that they should always keep their minds open for the direction the Lord has planned for them. At the end of that speech I read a poem I had written.

After the ceremony, a number of students came to cry on my shoulder. All I could do was hold them close and comfort them. These students may have talked with their parents initially after Stevie's death, but evidently they still held very deep feelings in their heart for him. The tears shed that evening cleansed the deep hurt in their hearts. As I talked to them, it was also very therapeutic for us, because we had to admit in front of everyone that our Stephen was no longer with us.

Perhaps you have had an opportunity to address a group function since your child died. When you did, I'm sure you could feel the love and support your listeners provided. It was a hurdle to cross, but the end result was love pouring from people who needed to show it and receive it. The Lord can use these times to bring to light His power and His compassion on those around us. He can use our strength and faith in Him to glorify His Name.

One can pursue many avenues in the area of memorials. We chose a few that had special meaning to us and our beliefs. We used money donated to the grade school for a memorial. We let the seventh grade decide what type of memorial they wanted to represent the love they had for their classmate. With the guidance of two seventh-grade teachers, they chose a beautiful, custom-made resurrection cross. It is black walnut with brass Easter lilies in the center. The background color of the cross changes with the seasons of the church year. It is placed over the entrance to the school cafeteria. Under the cross is a special plaque with the Bible passage: "I am the resurrection and the life" (John 11:25).

This was a meaningful way for the students to work on an outward expression of their grief. It also served as a reminder of their sorrow, their friend, and their faith. All of these feelings, happy and sad, come to mind as they look upon that cross each day.

We have also set up a scholarship program at the Lutheran high school where Stevie marched with the JROTC. It provides tuition assistance each year to a rifle squad member of JROTC who exemplifies Christian leadership. This scholarship is presented at a special dinner for endowed scholarship donors and recipients. It is a way to see your child's name remembered for generations to come and do it in a manner that helps further another child's education.

The Civil Air Patrol squadron Stephen was involved with set up its own honor cadet award in his name. This award is given to a cadet who best exemplifies the motivation, discipline, and characteristics of the Civil Air Patrol. The special part of this award is that it, like the seventh grade cross, originated with the friends who were part of Stephen's life. Every six months a cadet receives the award. We also provide, along with this award, a scholarship to be used for encampments and specialty schools for these young people.

Perhaps your child was involved in special clubs or organizations where you might donate a specific scholarship or award program. It is a wonderful expression of thoughtfulness in memory of your child. At the same time it contributes to the well-being of a young person and provides opportunities for him or her. The joy that you receive as these awards are given will open avenues for lasting friendships with each of the students receiving the honor.

On the home front, you can do material things to weave your way through the sometimes-tangled web of grief. A memory picture book will take some time to put together but will serve as a vivid reminder of the happy times of the past. Photographs are almost always taken when someone is smiling or having a great time. Putting all these pictures together in one book will give you hours of pleasure. Perhaps you would like to personalize it with a brass plate on the front with your child's name. You could also put in letters, cards, and mementoes from their friends. Pictures of the scholarship recipients can also go inside. Compiling these books will give you something to *do* with your grief. It will also provide other family members with quiet moments of remembrance when you are all together or when you are alone.

Another idea that anyone could do for his or her child, and which had a special meaning for us, was putting together a memory box. It is a framed box, about two inches deep, with a cloth background, covered with glass on the front. You can put in the memory box any items of remembrance from your child; perhaps ribbons or medals, maybe a picture or two that shows the child's personality and his special gifts from God. You may even want to put a little plaque with the child's name, birthdate, and date of death. We put our memory box on the wall in our family room. Maybe it is too soon for you to have pictures around the house, but when you are ready, you might consider a keepsake such as this.

Faith's Role

It is hard to imagine how anyone can go through the loss of a child without it affecting his or her faith. We all have to deal with death. We hope our children outlive us. As you already know, this is not always the way things happen. God has not promised that we would live a life of pure joy from beginning to end. The only joy He promised us was the joy of salvation through His Son, Jesus Christ. We are reminded of the passage told to us so many times as we have been nurtured in our faith:

> Jesus said, "Let the little children come to me, and do not hinder them, for the kingdom of heaven belongs to such as these." (Matt. 19:14)

This passage gives us that promise of eternal salvation for our souls and is especially mindful of children. Jesus has a special spot in His heart for children. When this passage was quoted, He even had to remind His most beloved disciples, the ones He chose, that the children were very close to his heart.

In John, Jesus talks about His sheep. As the Good Shepherd, He states:

My sheep hear My voice and I know them, and they
follow Me: And I give unto them eternal life; and they
shall never perish, neither shall any man pluck them
out of My hand. (John 10:27–28 KJV)

Jesus constantly refers to children as His little lambs
and to adults as His sheep. As a shepherd risks his life for
his sheep, so the Lord risked the life of His Son for all of us,
His sheep and lambs. We, by faith in Him, receive the ever-
lasting life that was purchased for us, and that hope holds
us together.

Let us hold unswervingly to the hope we profess, for he
who promised is faithful. (Heb. 10:23)

As you stand at your child's grave and are overwhelmed
with the sorrow, place your soul in the hands of Jesus, your
Shepherd. He will comfort you and place in your thoughts
the gift of eternal life that your child has received. Your
child is now where he has no more pain, no more sorrow,
no more tears, and the angels in heaven are watching him
so that he will never be alone. Our apprehension is that if
our child is not with us, he is afraid and alone. This is not
true in heaven. Jesus has placed your child in that special
mansion prepared for him. He will have more joy and friendship and love surrounding him than we could ever imagine
here on earth. And above all, he will have the peace we
strive for, the joy we long for, and the presence of our Savior before him always.

It is with this hope and faith that we survive. A parent
who loses a child has gained another treasure in heaven.
We have an inheritance waiting for us there in addition to
the glory of our Savior's throne. We cling to this as the days
grow weary for us, as our tears warm our cheeks, and as we

call to our Heavenly Father for strength. And He has replied:

> Even to your old age and gray hairs I am he, I am he
> who will sustain you. I have made you and I will carry
> you; I will sustain you and I will rescue you. (Isa. 46:4)

Prayer will become a lifeline for your spiritual and emotional well-being. Nothing has brought me to my knees in such intensity as the death of our son. Sometimes my prayers question why. Sometimes they are pleas for mercy and comfort for my grief. Sometimes they are petitions for God's love upon my child now with Him. And *always* they are cried in faith, believing they are heard by our Heavenly Father and that He will answer them. Through prayer we are not abandoned. We are one with Jesus and His love for us. He will give us the needed courage to live our days to His glory and reach that eternal and blessed reunion in heaven.

Journals, Pictures, and Poems

A number of people told me to write down my feelings on a daily basis after our son died. At first, this small task was much too painful for me. Just the thought of these painful feelings was too overwhelming, to say nothing about recording them on paper and thereby admitting that they not only existed, but that they were going to be a continued reality that I was not ready to accept. But as time went on, as with all things, it became easier to sort out my feelings. Eventually the web of confusion separated into defined thoughts and pictures that I found easier to describe on paper. I have a book with blank pages, and every now and then I filled in yet another happy memory of our son. The filled pages began to grow, and soon I looked forward to adding another and another happy remembrance. Some days I just sat and reread the pages and was surprised at how easily the smiles surfaced. Soon the entries brought laughter. Our whole family talked about the different scenes they witnessed and subsequently added even more "smiles" to the book.

Perhaps you are not ready to do this yet, but I encourage you to think about it for the future. You could incorporate so many remembrances about your child into a journal—his mannerisms, daily events, anecdotes, conversations, what made him smile. Each of these will help you to balance the sadness with brief moments of joyful memories. If your child were still here, he would also laugh at the things you found amusing and entertaining. The whole idea of a journal has a very therapeutic purpose not only for the parents but also for all the other family members.

Another activity that will help you to channel your grief in a constructive manner is to put together a special picture album. As you go through your current pictures and pull out special pictures of your deceased child, you will have your heartstrings tugged at frequently, I can assure you. But placing them in an album for you and family members to look at will also bring back special memories, and you will see the face of the one you love so dearly. You will be encouraged by the care and love you gave that child, and you will realize that you did the very best you could.

One family I interviewed, whose little girl lived only four days, put such a book together. The mother has one picture of the baby in an incubator where she is holding her daughter's tiny hand. When the picture was taken, the mother did not know that this was the last time she would touch her precious baby girl. This picture brings back some sorrow, but interestingly enough, as the mother showed this picture book to me—especially as she pointed out this picture—she had a smile on her face. She was so proud of her little girl. This picture had captured the one and only opportunity she had to touch her daughter, and it meant the world to her.

The little girl died in her father's arms at a children's hospital. The father has that picture in his memory. For this couple, the pictures in their "baby album" are all they have. Their child did not live long enough to receive awards or provide them with conversations and fun-filled memories as older children do. The parents of this baby, and others like her, hold this album as a precious part of their lives. This mother said that if they ever experienced a fire, this book would be the first item she would reach to save. I think every mother and father would say the same thing. It is the only lasting physical memory that parents have of their deceased child.

A memory book can also hold items other than pictures. Perhaps you have received some especially meaningful cards, personal notes, or even letters that have comforted you since your child's death. Putting them in an album where they are easily accessible can help you deal with a moment of pain that crept into your otherwise uneventful day. Perhaps you have just a minute to sit quietly and collect your thoughts. Maybe you need someone to encourage you, but no one is around. Turning to these thoughtful expressions of sympathy can give you the boost you need. Sometimes friends of your child will find it much easier to write you a letter to express their feelings than to visit you or call you on the phone. We received some wonderful letters from students who were quite shy and very quiet about their feelings. As we read through these letters, it warmed our hearts to know the impact our son had on their lives. It also helped us be thankful for the friendships that he had when he was alive and those which will be renewed in heaven.

Writing poems about your child and the grief associated with the death can be very helpful for some people. A number of books have prayers and poems written just for the grieving parents and family. Writing poems has been especially helpful to me. It is something that I enjoy doing, but in all humility I must admit that it does not come from my thoughts alone. Each time I write a poem, I pray for the Lord to use my pen to communicate His message. In no time at all, I have another poem. Without the Heavenly Father's wisdom, they surely would not be written. They are written for comfort and encouragement for anyone grieving the loss of a child. Many are written so that any parent could insert their child's name into the poem to personalize it and be refreshed and nourished by the Spirit of God and His message.

Grandchildren

If the child who has died is not an only child, parents will most likely have grandchildren. These grandchildren will provide the grieving families years of enjoyment and love. As you rest your eyes on a baby coming into this uncertain world from its secure shelter in the mother's womb, you can't help but be filled with emotion. Your thoughts turn to the plan for all our lives . . . a time to be born, a time to die. Your child left this world abruptly. Although this new baby could never replace that child, the Lord in His mercy has provided yet another avenue for you to channel your love and to experience joy.

As innocent and precious as they are, babies can impact your life without any effort on their part, or on your part, for that matter. Our Heavenly Father's love radiates from their presence to your heart. Other parents love and appreciate their grandchildren, but a grieving parent will embrace a silent prayer for the baby's welfare with a sincerity that is matched by no other.

Comforting Other Grieving Parents

During the past four years, we have been called upon many times to not only comfort other grieving parents, but in so doing, have been called to witness our Lord's mercy and grace throughout the grieving process. Each of the parents has dealt with the loss in their own unique way, but at the same time, similarities exist in all of them.

The parents who have recently gone through the devastation, generally within the first year, have the freshest pangs of sorrow and physical pain. They talk about the occurrence of their child's death, and the tears flow freely. The newness of the experience has dealt its overwhelming blow to their lives, and they grasp for answers and some type of accountability for the loss.

As we talk with parents in their second year of grief, they have accepted some of the pain, but with the second year comes new sadness in areas that during the first year provided only a numb background to the obvious emptiness. I asked a friend of mine during our second year of grief, "Why didn't you tell me that the second year posed new pain and was just as hard in some ways as the first?" She gently replied, "Because I had just finished my second year, and I didn't want you to lose hope." In her kindness, I soon realized that she was right to handle it the way she did.

Even though we have lost a part of our very self, even though we may not want to go on, and even though we feel as if we can never smile again, that little candlelight of hope still burns within each of us. I feel it is God's way of mending the torn dreams, healing the hurts within our hearts, and building us up even minutely day-by-day. The hope seems to be there even if we don't want it! The hope persists in coming to the surface more and more as time goes on. If you are not at a point where it has happened noticeably to you yet, be assured that it will. When it does, you will slowly, calmly, peacefully, and confidently deal with the grief that is before you.

The third year for us brought a greater acceptance, not without the sorrows, but the times of crying became less often and not as long. Some times of crying concluded with a fond memory or happy thoughts.

The fourth year presents more healing but not without moments when a tear unexplainably finds its way down the path of your cheek. But you are, nonetheless, healing. As time goes on, you rest your thoughts on that hope within you. For Christians, it is the hope of that reunion in heaven. It is the hope of a continued faith in our Savior and as a witness for all He has done and continues to do in your life.

As you comfort other families, a number of gestures and goodwill ideas can give them the support they need.

1. Being there for them at the time of their loss. Some very good friends of ours were standing outside the door of ICU the morning after our accident. They had lost a six-teen-year-old daughter in a car accident, and they knew the pain we were experiencing. I remember looking at them standing in that long hallway, by themselves, with tears in their eyes. They didn't have to say a word. I knew then, and only then, the pain they had gone through. The fact that they came to comfort us showed their unselfish and caring Christian nature. At that instant I knew that if they could live through this terrible pain, we could too. Just a tear shed in comfort, just your presence, can be the element of strength a newly grieving family may need. The sympathy expressed by a family that has gone through this pain contains a special meaning for those just going through it for the first time.

2. Stopping by to visit during the first few weeks and simply listening to them talk can help them work through their grief. They will know that although your child may have died differently, you have still experienced the same loss and you *know* how they feel. Any comforting words you can give them will be remembered.

3. Dropping a short note on the first anniversary of the child's death or on special days such as holidays, or birthdays, can give that warm arm of support and love they may desperately be needing on that day. Stores now carry cards that can be sent to someone who is not especially excited during the holiday season because of some loss in their lives. These meaningful cards can express your concern for them and assure them that they are in your thoughts and prayers during this difficult time.

4. Lastly, but certainly not least, you can pray for them. Who else on this earth knows the pain they are going through better than you? There have been days when we have felt an inner strength and wondered how we managed to make it through, only to find that a pastor or friend had said a special prayer for us on that particular day. Prayers are the building blocks upon which miracles are performed. Let the family know that you will pray for them and keep them in your thoughts. Then take it one step further and offer to be there for a call of consolation, anytime day or night. Just knowing there is always someone to listen can give you a sense of peace and take the sting out of the loss and loneliness.

Traditions

Traditions are avenues for parents who are trying to reestablish their lives within the family unit. Family gettogethers during holiday times or for special occasions can bring with them a very strong longing for the child who has been separated from your midst. In order to compensate for this obvious emptiness, traditions can be initiated not only to fill that emptiness but also to acknowledge the memory of that child in a way that not only helps the parents but also provides an outlet for other grieving family members.

Lighting a special candle during the traditional Thanksgiving dinner or Christmas Day feast can salute a moment of warm remembrance to each family member around the table without uttering a word. The candle can be lit before the family prayer or at the conclusion. Just the precious moment it takes to light the candle can bring each member together in spirit and reflection. Also helpful during a holiday, no matter what time of the year, is the planting of a tree in memory of your child. Besides helping the environment, you establish a living, symbolic ornament that will continue to provide beauty as the memory of your child lives on in your heart. Perhaps the brothers of the deceased child would like to dig the hole for the roots, and the sisters may want to help guide the tree into the ground. Family members should have their own special contribution in the planting of the tree. A discussion about traditions to be adopted would also bring each person into the planning process and give them a sense of ownership to the project.

Another family tradition that we have established gets its meaning from the afternoon before our son died. He had asked me to take him to the grocery store to get "lots of canned goods for the poor because there are a lot of poor people in our city." So off to the store we went. When we got home, we put the grocery bag of cans in the family room by the garage door, in anticipation of its arrival at school the next day. That evening Stephen went to be with his Heavenly Father, and the grocery bag stayed next to the door. In fact, it stayed there for months.

Finally one day we decided that it was not helping the poor by sitting there and that Stephen would have wanted that bag taken downtown to the church soup kitchen to be distributed. When we did this, we decided to establish a tradition with canned goods. Because Stephen died just before Christmas, and because he wanted the poor to have those cans before Christmas, we decided to give canned goods to the soup kitchen every year before the holiday and to put one small can in his stocking on the mantel. When we look at the stocking, we naturally think of the stocking hanging without our child's hand to reach inside, but we do have a warm feeling in our heart knowing that this little can symbolizes a generous gesture on his part right up until the time he died.

Your family can establish traditions that are pertinent to your lifestyle and beliefs. Perhaps you can incorporate another religious custom into a tradition of remembrance. Whatever theme you take, or whatever time you choose, it will work in healing the family as a whole. It acknowledges the loss by the unity in spirit and provides a ring of quiet comfort to each member.

Memory Tree

We've started some traditions since
you have moved away
To help us ease the pain that comes
without you here each day.
Can you peek down from heaven
and witness our loving acts
As we try desperately to blend
our memories with facts?
Our family traditions now include a little tree
That's planted every year for you;

it comes up to Dad's knee.
He digs the ground with careful skill,
each shovel brings to mind
A memory of innocence that's etched into his mind.
For his wish is that it should grow
to be so strong and tall
Much like the plans he had for you
before our Savior's call.
Your brothers place so carefully
the dirt around the base;
They do this slowly for they know
this is a special place.
The weather at Thanksgiving is now
turning bitter cold,
But they know that the time it takes
will help it to grow old.
When they are finished planting, it seems so very clear
That grief has had its purpose,
and they fight away a tear.
I witness this each season
as I peer through tear-filled eyes
For I can feel your precious smile come
shining through the skies.
This tree is a reminder of your new life, Stephen dear,
And we will plant one in your name
at just this time each year.
We've chosen here an evergreen;
its color does not fade,
Just as the love we have for you in this tree
is portrayed.

As the Hurdles Pass

Picture designed and created by Steve E. Kersey. Used with permissio

As the Hurdles Pass

As we continue in our daily life, has our view of the world changed at all since the death of our child? In all honesty, I think you will agree that it has. Our prayer life has intensified, and along with it has come requests for miracles. As we open our hearts to the Lord and His will, we can easily see miracles performed all around us. Some come as a result of our prayers, and some are unexplained. Only later do we find out that someone else has been keeping us in their prayers all along. Never underestimate the power of prayer. Its ray of hope brings with it wondrous events in the lives of all believers, but the Lord is especially compassionate with grieving families. His miracles become more evident as you open your heart and eyes to His Word.

Have your priorities changed since your child's death? From all the families I have interviewed, that question brought forth a resounding "Yes!" Each person affected by a child's death tends to intensify feelings of togetherness and love for family members and friends. One young man who was interviewed stated that he placed a greater importance on family relationships than he had before, not wanting to take anything for granted. He expressed this not only in his daily life but also in his essays at school and in his whole attitude about life. His faith was put on the line. He had to face the issue of a merciful God Who took his friend away suddenly, and a gracious God Who also provided that friend with a home in heaven, which is what he wants someday. The impact of one child's death can touch hundreds of lives in a way that it could not have living with us on earth.

As Christians, the values you instill in your children will also be met with more fervor and sincerity as you go down the path of grief and beyond. You will want to impress upon the siblings the importance of a faith in their Lord and Savior Jesus Christ for they may someday, without warning, also be taken to be with their Savior. You do not want to scare your child with the aspect of death, but you can gently instill in your children a love for their Savior that can take on new dimensions that were only glimpsed upon before this time.

As time goes by, your acceptance of your child's death will pave a pathway to healing and a renewed vision for your day-to-day activity and your future. Acceptance takes a very long time, and it can only be achieved by the Holy Spirit's power of healing and strength in your life. As you look toward your front door and see visions of your child entering, you will someday look and see only a door. Your child's voice will not ring through the hallway as it did for so many years. Those sparking eyes will not greet you as you rise to receive a hug. At first the thought of this instantly brings tears to your eyes and pain in your heart. But as time goes on, that vision will release the pain, and you will remember with joy that child coming through the door. That is when you will know that you are healing.

You will continue to move forward, almost without knowing it, but some days you will move backward. Expect those times and deal with them as I have suggested earlier in this book. But for each day or days backward, in the end you will feel a forward movement that indicates the grace of God is pulling you through yet another painful moment. I like to refer to all the painful times, those events that I can name specifically, as moving over "another hurdle toward heaven." That obstacle in front of us can toss us backward if we rely on our own energy. But if we ask for God's help as we begin that race and jump that hurdle, we will make it over the top. Remember, that hurdle is no more than the Lord will allow us to bear. And after we have crossed over it, we gain a sense of satisfaction in our hearts. We can say, "We did it!" Not of our own doing but with the help of Jesus.

Throughout this book, we have dealt with all the personal aspects of the grieving process. We have confronted the day-to-day twinges of pain that suddenly seem to invade our souls. We have prepared ourselves for upcoming holidays and special events in our lives. We have also confronted our grief on a family member and friend status. Each issue has presented, hopefully, a clearer understanding of what to expect as you travel down the path of separation from a loved one, a precious child. This book does not intend to provide a solitary means of support. It serves as a supplemental source of knowledge as to feelings and to reaffirm our Lord's plan in our lives. Along with this plan, He will provide hope and encouragement.

We cannot end the book without concentrating on our vision for the future, both for our families and ourselves. The Lord is too specific regarding His plan for our support to neglect its attention at this point.

Five main coping mechanisms are clearly intended for those grieving the loss of not only their child but anyone who was close to them.

1. *Patience.* The Lord has the following message of encouragement and patience for us:

> The Lord is good to those whose hope is in him, to the one who seeks him; it is good to wait quietly for the salvation of the Lord. (Lam. 3:25–26)

As you pass through your sadness, placing your hope in the Lord will bring compassion and goodness to you. As you seek His face through your tears, He has promised to bring His love upon you. He also tells us in this verse to patiently bear our sorrow, as we receive His grace, until we finally experience the salvation of the Lord. The Lord also says: "So do not throw away your confidence; it will be richly rewarded" (Heb. 10:35).

The Lord tells us to bear our cross patiently, do not lose faith, but continue our confidence in Him. With this confidence, He promises to richly reward us. That reward is our life in glory with Him—a life that will bring us fulfillment of our hope of heaven, a reunion with our loved ones, and the realization of being a member of God's heavenly kingdom.

The days after your child's death will turn slowly into years. You will feel the stronghold of your faith loosen in the beginning. But do not fear, the Lord knows your pain and heartache. As your hand loses its grip, His hand will hold on all the more firmly to guide you through your sorrow. He will use friends and family members to be extensions of His lovingkindness, and through them He will cradle you in a peace you have never known before—a peace that is completely dependent on Him and His will. As you see this outpouring of love in your life, you will slowly build up your faith again. Along with this renewed faith, you will reinvest your hope in a future that is not of this world but one that focuses on the goal of every Christian. That goal is living our lives for Christ here on earth and ultimately in heaven.

2. *Renewed Strength.* After our son died, a pastor in a nearby church spoke about strength. Some friends of ours attended that church and asked the pastor for a copy of that sermon. In the tape, he mentioned our loss. Although he had never met our family, his words of encouragement have been heard in our home many times. He quoted one Bible passage that has been of special comfort to me: "As your days are, so shall your strength be" (Deut. 33:25 KJV).

In this passage, the Lord tells us that He will provide just enough strength for the day. The sorrow or burden we carry, the hurt and pain we feel, will be in His hands. He will give us the strength to endure for that day. This is especially meaningful for grieving parents. Many days go by when we cannot see beyond the next minute or hour. We cannot comprehend what will happen the next day, or week, or month. We are too consumed with grief. As this grief takes over our souls, we have in this passage a renewed commitment from our Lord that He will constantly be our strength and will give us just the strength to get through the day. He alone knows what we have to face, and He alone gives us the ability to handle every minute. His promise not only applies to everyday events but also to our grieving hearts. He gives His power to heal our broken dreams and wounded souls. As a Shepherd gently cares for his sheep, He gently brings us back to life again. Focus on the passages below:

Though he brings grief, he will show compassion, so great is his unfailing love. (Lam. 3:32)

Because of the Lord's great love we are *not* consumed, for his compassions never fail. They are new every morning; great is your faithfulness. (Lam. 3:22–23)

These scriptures point us to the Lord's intention that our sorrows not consume us, great as the pain may be, but that His intention is to fill us with His compassion. This compassion is new to us every morning. His strength is renewed to us, given freely, out of His great love for us and through His understanding of our pain.

3. Stronger Faith. Did you consider yourself a Christian before your child died? I'm sure many of you questioned how God could bring this terrible pain upon you, knowing that you already belonged to Him. It isn't as if He had to strike you down to believe in Him. You have shown your love for Him many times through your commitment and Christian attitude. These questions are asked over and over by Christians as they experience the loss of their child. To further search for answers, we also declare that our child was a Christian who loved Jesus as His Savior. He could have brought so many more people to Christ by his lifestyle, by his witnessing. Lord, why did You take him? Have we had faith in a God who punishes the ones who love Him most?

There are no answers to these questions, and we would do best to accept them as unanswered issues until we meet our Lord face to face. Each of us will have a *long* list of questions that we will want answered. Until then we can reevaluate our faith as it is before us now. Upon doing so, and in the years to come, you will find that your faith has taken on a new perspective. You are evolving from a caterpillar into a butterfly. Your faith has taken on a new dimension in your life. As you have reached into the depths of your soul, as you have cried out in sorrow, you have also learned through your grief to place your entire being in His hands. You are too weak to face the world on your own, and you will find that hope in Him has given you the courage and strength that you need. As you realize this, your faith will become stronger and stronger in Him as the Lord of your life.

> May our Lord Jesus Christ himself and God our Father, who loved us and by his grace gave us eternal encouragement and good hope, encourage your hearts and strengthen you in every good deed and word. (2 Thess. 2:16–17)

4. *Wisdom.* Along with this faith will come wisdom to understand the will of the Lord for our lives. As Jesus said:

> Father, I want those you have given me to be with me where I am, and to see my glory, the glory you have given me because you loved me before the creation of the world. (John 17:24)

In this passage, Jesus says that it is His will that all believers be with Him in glory. That glory is God's heavenly kingdom. God wants each of us to have a place with Him in heaven. Knowing that our Lord receives us at death into His realm of glory gives us a peace that is surpassed by no other. The Lord intends for us to be there. He has prepared a place for us. When we die, we will worship our Lord in glory. What joy the wisdom of that hope gives us!

The apostle Paul wrote:

> Brothers, we do not want you to be ignorant about those who fall asleep, or to grieve like the rest of men, who

have no hope. We believe that Jesus died and rose again and so we believe that God will bring with Jesus those who have fallen asleep in him. (1 Thess. 4:13–14)

Here again, we are assured of the resting place of our child in heaven. God says in His Word that, as Christians, we have the hope of eternal life not only for ourselves, but we have the assurance that our loved ones who died in Christ will be with Him when they fall asleep. God assigned His only Son the death and resurrection for our souls. That act of complete love and redemption now gives us the peace that our child is cared for and endures every good thing.

5. *Vision.* As you look to the future, you have a vision ahead of you. You may not realize it, but by faith you possess it. It is a vision that produces joy out of your sorrow. As John writes: ". . . your sorrow shall be turned into joy" (John 16:20 KJV).

Even as your days are now filled with tears, we have the promise of eternal joy in heaven. This joy will include your child. If you wonder about the condition of your child in heaven, Jesus also gives us guidelines and a description of not only where they are, but how dear they are to Him. This is expressed in the following passage:

> See that you do not look down on one of these little ones. For I tell you that their angels in heaven always see the face of my Father in heaven. (Matt. 18:10)

We receive a very clear meaning as to the importance of children to our Savior. Not only do we know from the first sentence how much He loves them, but we are told that their angels always see the face of our Heavenly Father. We can assume they have a "front row seat" so to speak when it comes to making requests. This shows us also the importance our Heavenly Father places on those who care for children. Bringing them up in His Word and telling them of salvation through Jesus is to be foremost in their lives. Their care and well-being is so important to God that their angels always see God's face. What an elevation for our children!

To further assure us of the environment in heaven that surrounds our child, the Lord has also stated:

> He will wipe every tear from their eyes. There will be no more death or mourning or crying or pain, for the old order of things has passed away. (Rev. 21:4)

Ponder on My Presence

Ponder on my presence here in heaven's great domain,
Although I know you're wishing
that I could on earth remain.
But please be reassured for now, I'm in a special place
Right under Jesus' tender hand,
enveloped in His grace.
I see His face before me as I gaze in wonderment
And grasp His smile as I kneel down
with knees in earnest bent.
His loving power takes all my fears
and drives each one away
And this is where I comfort find and ever want to stay.
Maybe you fear I'm lonely, but that really isn't true
For angels gather round me;
we have many things to do.
Their kindness showers over me; I never am alone.
They tell me that they love me, too,
and that I here belong.
A warm and tender feeling seems
to fill the air up here,

And beauty glows around me and takes away all fear.
I smile each time I think of you
and all the ones behind,
But when they come to meet me here,
a joyful face they'll find.
The inner peace I share with others
gives my heart release
From pain and sorrow that you share
until you reach this peace.
And until you can make the journey
up through heaven's door,
I want you all to think upon the things
of love in store.
You'll come with open arms to me
and long for joys unknown,
And I can introduce you to our Savior in His home.
So until then keep smiling,
keep holding on with prayer,
And I'll be waiting, patiently,
as you live in His care.

Are you concerned as to the well-being of your child in heaven away from you and your special care? Rest assured that God is taking the best care of him. All the things in our lives that cause pain and sorrow, sickness, and even death are now passed away for our children in heaven. There is no more sorrow. There is only joy for our children. We cannot understand how they could experience complete joy if they are separated from our side, but the Lord tells us that He has made it all possible. Our Heavenly Father who loves us as His own children would never do anything to hurt those who love Him. Everything that comes upon us has happened for a reason, and nothing happens without first passing through our Father's hands. When He has taken our children into His nail-pierced hands, the same love He showed on the cross will continue to guide them through eternity.

Keeping this in mind, let's look at another passage written by Paul:

May the God of hope fill you with all joy and peace as you trust in him, so that you may overflow with hope by the power of the Holy Spirit. (Rom. 15:13)

As you ponder on this thought and see a regenerated faith and a clearer vision of your future in heaven, the Lord also guides us as He says:

You also must be ready, because the Son of man will come at an hour when you do not expect him. (Luke 12:40)

Just as the Lord took our child without warning, so we shall also enter the gates of glory. A sickness may give us a longer preparation time than dying in an accident, but nonetheless, we all shall go in the Lord's timing. As we reflect upon our child's death, we need to realize that our hearts should be ready also to receive the kingdom of heaven. Our Savior, and all those loved ones who have gone before, wait there for us. Our vision is a brilliant heavenly realm with Jesus before us and our loved ones at our side.

In closing, I would like to quote the words of Paul to the Ephesians. He had such a deep love and concern for them. That same bond is evident between families and friends who have lost a child. My prayer for you:

For this reason I kneel before the Father, from whom his whole family in heaven and on earth derives its name. I pray that out of his glorious riches he may strengthen you with power through his Spirit in your inner being, so that Christ may dwell in your hearts through faith. And I pray that you, being rooted and established in love, may have power, together with all the saints, to grasp how wide and long and high and deep is the love of Christ, and to know this love that surpasses knowledge—that you may be filled to the measure of all the fullness of God. (Eph. 3:14–19)

The Journey Home

Is there a future for me as I mourn
your death each day
Since Jesus called you to His side
and then took you away?
At first I thought I could not live my life
without you near,
But in my pain and sorrow,
Jesus wiped away each tear.
He came to sit beside me as I cried in silence torn;
He held my hand and lifted me
when I was weak and worn.
He seemed to whisper in my ear,
"I love you, too, My child,
Although I've taken one you love,
My care is meek and mild.
I'll wipe away each tear he quietly displays for you
And tell him that there is no deed for him
I would not do.
You must remember he's My own;
I gave new life to him.
The seed of faith within his heart,
I knew would never dim.
And you must keep this faith alive
as through each day you live
For I have blessings and a reservoir of joys to give.
I need you now to tell the ones
who suffer with the same

That I have kept their little ones;
I've given them My name.
I'm counting on you to hold fast as you recall My love
And hold My promise in your heart,
until we meet above.
So until then your child
and I will guide you through each day,
Until we meet you at our gate and there forever stay."

To contact the author for speaking engagements or for a brochure of other Faith Petals items, please write to:

Jean Werth
Faith Petals, Inc.
3207 Joshua Ct.
Highland, IL 62249

Or visit online at:
www.FaithPetals.com

To order additional copies of

There's Someone in Your KINGDOM, Lord

order online at www.FaithPetals.com

Bookstores may place orders through:

Pleasant Word
PO Box 428
Enumclaw, WA 98022
Fax: 360-802-9992
Phone: 360-802-2907

Printed in the United States
54097LVS00001B/367-414